Poems of Wine and Tavern Romance

GLOBAL ACADEMIC PUBLISHING

Volume III in the Series: East-West Bridge Builders

Poems of Wine and Tavern Romance

A Dialogue with the Persian Poet

Hafiz

Translated, with verse replies and commentary, by

Martin Bidney

State University of New York Press

Cover illustration by Annie Johnson

Published by
State University of New York Press, Albany

Printed in the United States of America

For information, contact
State University of New York Press, Albany, NY
www.sunypress.edu

Production, Laurie Searl
Marketing, Michael Campochiaro

Library of Congress Cataloging-in-Publication Data

Bidney, Martin.
Poems of wine and tavern romance : a dialogue with the persian poet Hafiz / Martin Bidney.
pages cm. — (East-West Bridge Builders ; Volume III)
Includes bibliographical references and index.
ISBN 978-1-4384-4789-6 (hardcover : alk. paper) 978-1-4384-4788-9 (pbk. alk. paper)
1. Hafiz, 14th cent.—Influence. 2. Hafiz, 14th cent.—Appreciation. 3. East and West in literature. I. Title.
PK6465.Z8316 2013
891'.5511—dc23 2012045700

10 9 8 7 6 5 4 3 2 1

I dedicate my book to

Katharina Mommsen and Khalil Semaan,

who by their kindness, wisdom, and encouragement

have helped empower me for this endeavor.

Contents

*I want to express the deepest gratitude to co-editor James Peltz,
project editor Laurie Searl, copy-editor Catherine Chilton,
and graphic artist Annie Johnson.*

East-West Introduction

Hafiz, Hammer, Goethe

As in medieval times, the culture of Iran today is poetry-loving to a degree hard to conceive in the West. My son-in-law's brother travels widely in the Middle East. Recently he was in Isfahan on a Friday night, where men gathered at a crossroads to recite and hear, for their evening entertainment, favorite poems of Persian poet Muhammad Shemseddin Hafiz (ca. 1320–1389). Here in Binghamton, New York, I cannot imagine high school or college people, or any other group, spontaneously congregating downtown on State Street to declaim, let's say, Dante (1265–1321) or Chaucer (ca. 1343–1400) or any other poet, medieval or modern. To enter the spirit of this Persian master, of his cultural and religious world, has meant, for at least one present-day adventurer, to encounter an uncommonly intense poetic life. A dialogue with Hafiz' poems, read in the German translation by Joseph von Hammer that stimulated J. W. von Goethe, Germany's greatest poet, to write his own influential book of lyrical replies proved transformative for me and perhaps may have an enlivening effect on others. Hammer and Goethe are engaging mediators, and I will invoke their aid in my brief introduction to Hafiz' lyrical achievement.

This book is an East-West "dialogue" of three kinds. To list them will be helpful in providing background for the unusual and in some ways pathbreaking project I undertake.

1. I am a dialogic translator: I re-sing works by lyric masters of unusual appeal (Goethe, Mickiewicz; see Goethe 2010, Bidney 2007) so I can learn their favored musical forms, use them in my verse "replies," and thus carry on a verse dialogue with the poetic mentor. My teacher

here is Hafiz (as interpreted via Hammer), and you will find that all the re-singings of him in this book aroused dialogic responses from me. By reading my rendering of each Hafiz-Hammer lyric together with the juxtaposed reply, you will obtain interpretive commentaries on the Persian poet's religious and legendary allusions, often with supplements of varied kinds (e.g., songs from Ovid's *Amores*, Horace's *Odes*, and the medieval *Carmina Burana*).

It is a particular pleasure to converse, in poems, with Hafiz, for he has the complexity of a character in Shakespeare: he can be vigorous, tender, defiant, repentant, despairing, fanciful, meditative, witty, playful. And no matter what calamities may arise from the cruelty of rulers and the fickleness of lovers, the Persian craftsman draws unfailing sustenance from the scripture-influenced metaphoric music deployed to chronicle his energetic life of sensuality and spirit. Revered in Iran today as oracular, a numinous figure whose poems, randomly chosen, are considered aids to fortune-telling, Hafiz celebrates the delights, and laments the woes, of wine and tavern romancing in a heady atmosphere of Qur'anic, mythic, and bold Sufi allusion (or, when reckless, anti-Sufi protest—for we meet here a most rebellious monk).

2. The version of the book from which I selected 103 poems to render, a German translation of the *Divan* of Hafiz, is itself already an intercultural breakthrough, an East-West dialogue of a striking kind. It is the pioneering German version of Hafiz' *Divan* by Joseph von Hammer (or Hammer-Purgstall), the first translation of Hafiz' complete *Divan* into any European language (Wohlleben 2004, 11). Hammer has made of Hafiz' Persian work a cornucopia of unexpected metrical forms, a festival of rhythms that is one of the finest musical achievements I have ever had the good fortune to enjoy. Hammer employs innumerable rhythmic patterns, often classical but also of his own design, which I have emulated with alacrity. Hammer's rhythmic genius has never been adequately recognized, in Germany or anywhere else, and in the present volume I hope to remedy this neglect. Unearthing a forgotten cache of musical experiments, I have tried to show how the appealing inventions made by the German metrist are ready for use by poets today.

3. Most important of all from a broad global standpoint, Hammer's German rendering of Hafiz' Eastern *Divan* (see Hafis [1814] 1973) in his unique Western mix of classical and invented meters was the overpowering stimulus for Goethe's *West-East Divan* of 1819, a pioneering intercultural dialogue in verse that I translated in volume II

of this Bridge Builder series (see Goethe 2010). Goethe (in a lyric I cite below) called Hafiz his "twin," and this twinship is one of the most curious and meaningful relations in the history of literature. As I translated and replied to Hammer's Hafiz while creating the book you are now holding, I often had in mind Goethe's responses to his Persian brother, and sometimes Goethe is introduced, also, in my verse commentaries. The implications of Goethe's encounter with Hammer-and-Hafiz in his own poetic evolution cannot be overestimated, as Katharina Mommsen has shown in a series of brilliant scholarly works over many decades (e.g., *Goethe and Islam* [2001]). To bring Hammer's Hafiz alive for today's English-speaking reader is to re-open in yet another way the East-West dialogue that Goethe initiated nearly two centuries ago when he wrote his German-Persian book in reply to Hammer's.

Very little is known of Hafiz' life: even A. J. Arberry's "barest outline" (1962, 2–8) and Wohlleben's biographic summary (2004, 9–11) tell mainly about fourteenth-century Persian heads of state. But Hammer, basing himself on both text and legend, was right to point out the poet's defiance of ostensible, or ostentatious, power. In his glowing preface, Hammer writes:

> Honored by princes, loved by friends, Hafiz, in the rose gardens of Shiraz, passed in pleasure and study the days of his life, during what happens to have been one of the stormiest centuries Oriental history had ever known. Dynasties moved to battle by mutual hatred arose in succession, one upon the ruins of the other, each to fall in its turn, yet all eager to raise the firebrand of war, until by the all-conquering brand of Timur the entirety of Asia lay in flames—an encompassing and fearful conflagration. Hafiz was presented to the Emperor, who received him with grace, although in one of his *ghazals* he had gone so far as to dismiss Samarkand and Bokhara, the chief adornments of the crown of Timur, as of less worth than a beauty mark of his [male] beloved.
>
> The horror of the political storms that had convulsed the Orient offers a notable contrast to the untroubled serenity of the poet who, while realms collided round him and usurpers shot upward in thunder, sang with unruffled cheer of nightingale and rose, of wine and love. The fury of the times must have freed a spirit like that of Hafiz for an even greater liberty than would have been possible in a more tranquil era.

> Had he waited to sing immortal songs until peace and rest arrived, the songs would have remained unsung and his name would not hover today in the Orient with high inspiration on every lip, while the names of Jenghiz Khan, Timur, and Nadirshah are preserved by history only as a scar on humanity, a warning and a sad example to future generations. (Hammer, "Vorrede," in Hafis [1814] 1973, xxx–xxxi)

The lyric that reportedly got Hafiz into trouble with Timur (or "Tamerlane"—the "Tamburlaine" satirized by Christopher Marlowe in his play of that title) is poem 8 in the present collection. In part 1 of my verse "Reply," I tell the legend in more detail, borrowing from Hammer's entertaining narrative, and in part 2 I write my own hymn of praise to Hafiz, versifying and expanding Hammer's moving peroration. Katharina Mommsen has persuaded me that it was probably this Hammer passage that most vividly kindled the enthusiasm of Goethe for his long-hidden "twin." The German poet, too, exasperated and perplexed by the collision of realms around him in the Napoleonic Wars in 1814, looked, as did Hafiz, for an unfettered exercise of his talent in what would prove a life-restoring relief from a noxious political atmosphere.

Parallel to the Hammer quotation, on the other side of our entryway to the work of Hafiz I would like to place Goethe's own evaluation of the Persian poet's achievement, from the "Notes and Essays" section of his *West-East Divan* (also included in volume 2 of the Bridge Builders series, this prose document was translated by me and Peter Anton von Arnim; see Goethe 2010). Goethe's comment, too, owes plenty to Hammer, this time to his richly informative *Arts of Eloquence in Persia* (1818):

> If a brother in faith earned the greatest merit in reproducing a copy of the Qur'an or in having it copied, it was no less a merit to learn it by heart so that on any occasion one might quote the appropriate passages, to promote edification or to settle a dispute. Such persons were given the honorific title *Hafiz*, and this remained with our poet as the principal name to designate him.
>
> . . . A truly intelligent, sensible man had to make every effort to return to the original, pure text, and they did so. That is why in the history of Islam we find interpretation, application, and practice often worthy of admiration.

It was for such a skill that the finest poetic talent was trained and educated. The entire Qur'an belonged to him, and no religious edifice founded on it was secret to him. He himself says,

"Due to the Qur'an alone
Is whatever I've achieved."
(mim 43, 39, in Hafiz 2, 223)

In his hometown Shiraz, to which he limited himself, he taught as dervish, Sufi, and sheikh, well liked and highly regarded by the Muzaffar family and their connections. He was occupied with theological and grammatical works and rallied a large number of disciples.

To these serious studies, involving the holding of a teaching post, his poems stand in total contradiction, which might be resolved, however, if we say: the poet must not believe in and live everything he expresses, least of all the poet who, born in a later period, gets into complicated circumstances requiring him to assume a rhetorical disguise and to present what contemporaries want to hear. That was the case with Hafiz. . . .

I will say but little about these poems: one should enjoy them and bring oneself into harmony with them. A tempered, yet upwelling vitality streams from each. Unassumingly happy and judicious within limits, taking part in the fullness of the world, looking into the mysteries of the divinity from afar, but also at one point rejecting religious practice as well as sensual pleasure, the one as much as the other—so in general this kind of poetry, whatever it appears to promote and teach, must above all maintain a skeptical mobility. (Goethe 2010, 202–203)

"Upwelling vitality" and "skeptical mobility"—not a bad personality sketch of either the Persian poet or his German brother. The related phrase "poet-spring/That wave on wave unnumbered up will fling," suggesting vitality combined with mobility, appears in the poem to Hafiz (which I will quote in a moment) that Goethe entitled "Unbounded." And so does the fascinating enigma at the heart of Goethe's above-cited depiction of his friend, the idea of a "total contradiction" between the serious theological studies of Hafiz, the "religious practice" of the honorifically named Qur'an memorizer, and his unquestionable devotion to "sensual pleasure." This is indeed the polarity—the tension, conflict, or ambivalence—that needs to be spelled out. Put bluntly, the Qur'anic metaphors in Hafiz' lyrics are evoked by two urgent and constant worldly concerns: wine and tavern romance. In his lyrics on Hafiz, Goethe tends to reconcile hedonism and the ideal, portraying the Persian singer as wholly at home in a world instilled with vital energies. But, as we will see later, powerful tensions erupt.

"Unbounded" is the Goethean lyric to Hafiz that, of all the tributes to him in the "Book of Hafiz" within *West-East Divan*, most helpfully embodies the polarity of passion and higher insight, although here Goethe doesn't present it as any sort of conflict but rather as an encompassing range, a plenitude. First we have a strophe that makes the Persian singer seem godlike, *sphaera cuius centrum ubique,* a sphere whose center is everywhere. The perfectly integrated, unified Hafizian "song" that Goethe mentions here can only refer to the poet's total work, viewed as one lifelong literary confession:

> That you can make no ending makes you great;
> That you have no beginning is your fate.
> Your song turns round, a star-vault heaven-frame;
> Beginning, ending, evermore the same;
> And the clear import of the middle part
> Is present at the end, as at the start. (Goethe 2010, 23)

Goethe liked to view his own works as constituting a single confession in this Hafizian way (cf. Wohlleben 2004, 42). The wording might also make it appear as if Hafiz' individual poems were models of unity, perfect microcosms of the macrosphere. But that idea is belied by the facts: the ghazal, Hafiz' favored lyric form, prizes the organic unity of each individual two-part verse, but not of the larger poetic whole, and Hafiz' poems in the present collection often ramble. It was precisely this rambling quality that made it easy for subsequent poets to tack on, or insert, their own unrequested supplements or even, very often, to scramble the ordering of the couplets or to alter them further, deliberately or in error, making the establishment of a canonical Hafizian text an unrealizable ideal (Arberry 1962, 10–12). Even a scrupulous, cleaned-up text like that prepared by the excellent present-day scholar Joachim Wohlleben continues to offer sequences of couplets (long two-part verses) that unexplainably digress or suddenly shift in focus. Indeed, the often disjointed structure of the ghazals has had the effect of dramatizing the wild mood swings that are a daily part of the poet's love travail. There is a reckless impulsivity in him that may in part justify the parallel drawn in poem 44 to Mejnun, the Romeo of Persia, who, exiled from his native city by his ladylove's father (a member of a rival family), writes the fair one's name tirelessly in the sand, only to have it swept away each time by desert winds.

The inclusive exuberance of Hafiz' poetic personality, lauded in strophe 1 of Goethe's tribute poem, exemplifies that plenitude in devotion to love and wine in strophe 2:

> Of joys you are the truest poet-spring,
> That wave on wave unnumbered up will fling,
> Lips ever ready for a kiss,
> From ardent breast a hymn that flows,
> Throat eager for the drinker-bliss,
> A kind, outpouring heart that glows. (Goethe 2010, 23)

The wine, the hymn, the heart of love conspire. And Goethe will offer his own love testament:

> Should the whole world to ruin sink,
> Háfiz, with you, with you alone
> I'd vie! Desire and painful moan—
> We'll share them both, we twins have grown!
> To be like you in love, in drink—
> My pride, my life in this be shown!

The final couplet of the poem is a supplementary, paradoxical tribute:

> My song, your fire's unique to you!
> You have united old and new.

Here Goethe praises the poem he has just written: how can this be called a tribute to Hafiz? Yet if imitation is sincerest flattery, the tacked-on two-liner is a high compliment. For Hafiz loves to end a ghazal by turning from the topic at hand to wind up his performance with a postscript couplet of self-praise. The tactic is a trademark of his, and you will encounter it repeatedly.

"Open Secret" allows Goethe to comment once more on sense and spirit in Hafiz, and again he views them as integrated, not divided. The plenitude of Hafiz' personality fascinates him:

They've claimed you, holy Hafiz,
A mystic tongue command.
These men of words, however,
That word don't understand.

They call you "mystic," thinking
Their nonsense-thought—for shame!
While impure wine they're drinking
And serving in your name.

But you're pure, and *mystically*.
Yet they cannot make it fit
That you're blest without any piety!
And this they will *not admit*. (Goethe 2010, 25)

"Unbounded" and "Open Secret" together portray a Hafiz thoroughly at home in the world, not "pious" before a transcendent sovereign of the universe but blessed in a mystical oneness with all that is—a temperament more deeply rooted in him than a doctrine, a state of mind rather like the *hen kai pan* or "all in one" mentality of Goethe himself.

This reconciling oneness allows Goethe, in a third and crowning lyric tribute, to transform Hafiz into the priest of a wine religion based on a delightful comic re-envisioning of scripture:

Create and Enliven

Jack Adam was an earthly clod
That God a man would make.
But certain things uncouth and odd
From mother-womb he'd take.

The Elohim into his nose
The best of spirits blew,
At which improved respect arose.
He sneezed—and that was new.

With bones and limbs and head on top
He stayed half clod, not whole,
Till Noah for the needed drop
Had found the needed bowl.

The clump feels, right away, the swing,
Soon as he tastes the wet,
Much as the dough, when leavening,
In motion will be set.

So let us all your holy song
And model, Háfiz, heed:
With drink in clinking goblets strong,
To Heaven's temple lead. (Goethe 2010, 8–9)

Hafiz' poem 62 ("Listen!—for what is the call from the merchant of souls at the market?") is but one of many that could have stimulated the composition of this hymn to the clinking goblets. And poem 52 ("Friends! what a penance the vine's lovely daughter has done!"), with its monorhyme "done" at the end of every couplet as required by the Hafizian ghazal form, sets the model not only for the alcoholic content but also for the surprising monorhyme fidelity we discover in yet another fine Goethean tribute-piece—this one implicit, as the Persian poet is not named:

Folks have, regarding drunkenness,
Found fault with us before
And are, about our drunkenness,
Ready to say much more.
Generally, a drunkenness
Will down you till the dawn.
But here, at night, my drunkenness
Hunted me, on and on.
It is my lover-drunkenness
That plagues unmercied makes;
From day to night, from night to day
Dismays a heart that quakes,
A heart, that in a drunkenness
Of swelling singing plays—
Of *that*, no sober drunkenness
Can wanted warning raise.
Love-, song- and wine-made drunkenness
Whether by day or night—
Ah, the divinest drunkenness
Will plague me—and delight! (Goethe 2010, 129)

Again the principle of plenitude is lauded without stint, as wine becomes the symbol, for Goethe as it is for Hafiz, of all divine inebriations, including poetic madness and the prime mover, love.

Goethe has come closer here, perhaps, than anywhere in his work to achieving the perfect embodiment of Hafizian poetic ardor, while also employing a more or less Hafizian ghazal-like form, with monorhymed endings in two-part verses. Hammer had demonstrated how one might set about writing ghazals: see poem 52, cited above; poem 12 ("I said to the King of Beauty"); or poem 67 ("'Mid handsome ones I'm famous, faithful as the candle"). Goethe was so excited by them that in "Emulation," he sets up ghazal writing as his own Hafizian ideal of poetic form:

> I'm hoping that I learn to write with ease
> Using your rhyme-form, repetition, too.
> First meaning, then the word I'll seek, to please;
> Let any end-tone that returns to view
> Deepen the meaning innovatively.
> No one more gifted at this feat than you.
>
> For as the spark enkindling—rapidly—
> Moscow, when horrid rising flames climbed round,
> Aroused more wind, by heated winds blown free,
> Then vanished, quelled, to higher star-hall bound,
> From you came forth eternal glowing gold,
> A German heart to liven and make bold. (Goethe 2010, 24)

It is an alluring, endearing vision: to use repetitive Persian-style end rhymes with continually new shifts of implication that deepen the meaning while displaying unexhausted originality. But in German, or English, it's a formal aim nearly impossible to achieve. Goethe's own "Highest Favor" (2010, 50), with its repetitions of the line-ending "found," is not one of his best. Realizing this, perhaps, he rarely tried ghazals again.

Now, I think, we can begin to see what motivated Hammer, in his Hafiz translations, to compose so rarely in ghazal-like form and instead to experiment widely with meters that would work better, in his own language, to convey the plenitude of being, the fullness of life, that he, and later Goethe, found in the Persian master. Hammer's renderings were by no means perfect; all commentators agree that he worked far too rapidly, and Wohlleben (2004, 13) even calls his work "slapdash." But the Hafiz renderings that Wohlleben likes best, those with "pleasantly paired rhymes" in the "extremely rare" edition of the *Divan* by Rosenzweig-Schwannau (1858-1864), he all the same dismisses with faint praise: "metrically smooth," he calls them, never "vigorous," and he warns today's reader of their "hopelessly antiquated" diction (Wohlleben 2004, 15–16). The fifty poems in A. J. Arberry's (1962) reputable compilation (the better ones, as he says, were translated by Gertrude Bell [Hafiz 1928]) are in every kind of meter. They are as much the renderers' own inventions as are the experiments of Hammer, but, if elegant, show far less verve. It is clear that one had best be ingenious and resourceful in seeking solutions to the intractable problem of finding English verse forms adequate to convey induplicable Persian ghazals (for the complexity of the difficulties, see Parvin Loloi 2004, 3–21).

I have not hesitated to adopt the Hammer example, for it is the one that awakened me to the abundance of life in Hafiz' work. I do take seriously, however, Wohlleben's warnings about Hammer's inaccuracies. So, whenever possible, I have checked him against Wohlleben's careful word-for-word prose translations, and I've emended many phrases accordingly. Wohlleben has helped make my renderings clearer and more accurate, although of course innumerable subtleties are missed, something that cannot be helped. No one will ever copy the clever Persian-language wordplay.

Also owing to Wohlleben, my English Hafiz will offer one big surprise. Hammer, in 1814, had Hafiz writing love poems mainly to women, but Wohlleben, in 2004, makes it clear that the overwhelming number of addressees were men (and he notes that Rosenzweig-Schwannau had already revealed this in 1858). Hammer censored Hafiz. I, following Wohlleben, have restored accuracy and candor. But Hammer's distortions were not comprehensive: in the anecdote narrated above, he makes it clear that Hafiz had claimed in his poem that he would gladly trade Samarkand and Bokhara for the beauty mark of his *boy*friend ("seines Lieblings"). Poem 8, the lyric in which the topic of the trade is broached, spells out in more detail the attractions of handsomeness. And poem 18 ("See the swarthy one? Look") offers another example of many poems about beauty marks or moles that might be cited to reinforce the point I'm making. Like Hafiz, Goethe portrays homoerotic sentiments in the following exchange, in *West-East Divan*, between Poet and Cupbearer:

To the Cupbearer:

You charming boy, come right inside:
Why do you stand at the entrance there?

You'll be my cupbearer!—by my side—
And every wine will be fine and fair.

Cupbearer speaks:

You, there, with the light brown curls,
Go away, you artful Miss!
Master thanks me when I serve,
And my forehead gets a kiss.

You, though, I would have to bet,
Couldn't be content with this.
Overeager cheeks and breasts
Wearily will he dismiss.

Do you think you're fooling me
When you leave, ashamed? I'll lie
On the threshold and awake
When I feel you gliding by. (Goethe 2010, 128)

Hafiz does at times write moving lyric tributes possibly addressed to women: Persian pronouns leave the question open. Poem 66 ("The sweet, alluring charm of your face had seized"), framed in the finest alcaic rhythm, ends memorably:

For you, O Háfiz, 'twere but an idle act
To kiss the dust of earth at the feet of her—
    The raving tale of all your longing
        Told by the clamoring winds about you.

And I love the depth, as well as the "mobility," of the many-strophe'd poem 29 ("While your image sways before me"), as here:

Woe! she's fled and gone, the dear one.
And my eyes in tears are swimming,
With the beauteous form that wavers
Painted on the flowing water.

Or here, in the delightfully unexpected ending:

O you fiery seed of heart-flame,
I, unfed by face-light gleaming,

See my heart, a heated dancer,
Long ago to dust-heap crumbled.

Yet may Háfiz still be drunken,
Roving-eyed and freely dreaming,
For with many bits of mischief
Is our time of youth enlivened.

But even when Wohlleben decides to interpret a pronoun as feminine, he adds a footnote explaining that the Persian text leaves the matter unclear: the addressee might just as well be male. I follow his decisions regarding gender in these debatable cases, as in all others.

Goethe, in his Persian lyric persona, presents himself as bisexual. (Indeed, Katharina Mommsen, in a book whose English title would be *No Means of Rescue But Love* [2010], shows the power of homoerotic sentiment in the poet's own life vis-à-vis Friedrich Schiller.) The matter is dramatically summed up in the following outburst:

That vile trollop,
A temptress,
"World," as they call her—
She's cheated me
As she did all the others:
Took away Faith,
Then Hope,
Now she wants
To grab Love—
But I snatched it away;
To secure forever
The treasure I'd saved,
Dividing it wisely
Between Zuleika and Saki—
Each of the two
Kept busy competing
For maximum profit.
Yet I'm richer than ever!
I've got my Faith back! (Goethe 2010, 132)

Hafiz, for his part, recurrently employs two strategies to promote unfettered self-expression in his passionate avowals: (1) rhetorical open-endedness regarding the sex of the addressee and (2) an atmosphere of androgyny in the depiction and metaphoric evocation of the beloved.

The Persian poet is wholly absorbed by the experience of love in its interiority: love itself is what matters, far more than the gender of the love object. Typical is poem 70 ("So long as on my head your shadow falls," rendered by Hammer as a blank verse sonnet): in English, unlike German, even the word "friend" in line 10 is not gendered, so you have to wait till the final couplet to learn—or, more precisely, to guess by way of the implications of male words such as "Shah" and "Vizier"—that the friend is a man.

What made it so easy for Hammer to bowdlerize Hafiz by altering only a word here and there is that young men in Persian lyrics have ruby lips, fragrant tresses, a tiny waist, narcissal eyes. The narcissus, related to the daffodil, has no features that would clearly resemble a human ocular pupil, but the frilly ruffle surrounding the opening of the calyx might well suggest long, thick, rounded lashes. In a recurrent dialogue of flowers, the friend is a rose and the poet is a Turkish-style elongated tulip, red with passion but exhausted or burnt out with unrequited longing, pictured with what looks like an extinguished candlewick at the center of the flower.

Shakespeare, we may recall, began his *Sonnets* with a poem likening his friend to a rose. The pervasive androgyny of Shakespearean imagery in this work will seem entirely natural to the Hafiz reader (see my verse commentaries to poems 39, 41, 45, and especially, for Shakespeare, the detailed "Reply" to poem 50). Spring winds are joyful or disheartening, depending on whether they bring, or fail to convey, the rich poppy aroma of the comrade's hair. It was clever of Hammer to employ, with avidity and skill, classical Theocritan-Ovidian elegiac distichs or couplets. These beautiful conversational forms, with their casual ease, accomplish a valuable twofold purpose: (1) to represent the two-part structure of the long Hafizian ghazal-verse, or *beit,* and (2) to convey the fact that the homoerotic attraction so often called "Greek love" could just as well be styled "Persian love" in these poems. Readers of Homer, as of Vergil, Horace, or Catullus, will understand cupbearer and poet in the context of youthful Ganymede and Jupiter or Zeus.

But we will never get to the heart of Hafiz' poetry until we pass beyond the undeniably attractive and prominent "upwelling vitality" and "skeptical mobility," the principle of plenitude, as it were, that Goethe emphasized in his lyric tributes. For both wine and homoerotic passion, Hafiz' two predominant loves in worldly life, stand in "contradiction" to the religious concerns of his professional life, as Goethe also recognized. Both of these worldly predilections are subjected to strictures in the Qur'an, although there are debates, within Islamic tradition as a whole, about how severely or leniently the prohibitions are to be interpreted. Wine in particular seems to have got Hafiz into trouble with fellow blue-cowled monks in the Sufi order to which he belonged, not to mention the far more stringent rule enforcers enrolled in the Wine Police under Mubariz ud-Din. (What a blessed relief for the poet when the alcohol-tolerant Shah Shuja comes to power!—see poem 65.) In the *West-East Divan* lyric beginning "True predominance, you'll feel," we see Goethe identifying sympathetically with a fellow victim of social pressures:

> Háfiz, Ulrich Hutten too,
> Warded off their foes who took
> Symbol-cowls of brown or blue;
> Mine like other Christians look.
>
> "Name them, then—the enemy!"
> No, we'll leave the matter there.
> They, in our society,
> Gave me quite enough to bear. (Goethe 2010, 56)

But Hafiz appears more abject, more pathetic in many of his own self-portraits as tavern thrall than in these somewhat idealizing lines by his admirer. In poem 32 we hear him say,

> The marks of wine that spatter my cowl
> I'd wash away with tears if I could.
> The age of moderation has come—
> A season for fasting.

Yet, even here, Hafiz will not apologize to anyone. He ends the poem with his trademark strophe of self-praise as conqueror, in song, of the realms where his dignity has been questioned. But the point is made: the life of the Persian singer is one of dualities, contradictions—and these lend even more life to his writing. His energies, unquellable, are daily tested.

Part of the key to his triumph is summed up in the honorific name "Hafiz," meaning one who has the holy scripture by heart. (Recall the couplet Goethe cited: "Due to the Qur'an alone/Is whatever I've achieved.") Whether love and wine have made him their hapless victim, their holy martyr, or their triumphant embodiment, the poet can find Qur'anic parallels for his longing, his suffering, and his victory. He will be larger than life insofar as he can equate his life to that of a universal pilgrim, fallen but redeemable. Of course our empathy or sympathy, if not lessened, will be lightened or leavened by the manifest ironies we relish, felt sharply or amusedly by the poet himself, in all of the transformations where we see the toper, the amorist, the tireless lover of pleasure portrayed as Noah, Joseph, Solomon, Alexander, Jesus, Zoroaster—not to mention Simurg or Anka, mythic birds of wisdom, longevity, rebirth.

But often, the contrast between the pitiful condition of the drunken, lonely, derelict monk and his purported Qur'anic or folkloric ideal prototype is so glaring, the gap so wide, that the incongruity provokes laughter or a smile. We may be simultaneously moved and bemused. Traditional Persian critics have not wanted to dwell on the frequently comic disparities. Rather, throughout the centuries, we find a fraternal collusion of poet and interpreter who will promote mystical readings and religious allegories in quite a sober frame of mind. The mole on the face of Hafiz' boyfriend has been equated to an ink dot in the Holy Qur'an. Gertrude Bell (Hafiz 1928, 152) is right to be a bit sarcastic about this. Yet perhaps we need not be startled by it: a parallel opinion maintains, in traditional Hebrew and Christian readings of the biblical Song of Songs, that this overwhelmingly erotic work, one of the most devoted pictorial-melodic celebrations of physical love in all of world literature, must in some way be an allegory of higher things in the world of the unseen. And once that equation is made, the traditional commentator will not readily descend from the spiritual level to consider, in its own terms, the earthly or earthy one. Wohlleben would advise us not to choose between material and mythical interpretation in reading the lyrics of the Persian master: it is a false choice, for both are co-present. Hafiz, he tells us, wanted his work to be maximally ambivalent so that it would be possible to read images or episodes as sensory and suprasensory at once; the great Orientalist-poet Friedrich Rückert, he adds, had made the same point (Wohlleben 2004, 41–42).

That is true and valuable, if interpreted in a rather general way, but we must go farther. Modern readers, schooled by Shakespeare, will rarely see everything in a Hafiz poem as equally two-sided. Instead, they will most greatly relish, in the varied or mingled moods, either from poem to poem or within a given lyric, the *altering proportions* of bodily indulgence and mystical dreaming, of hyperbolic elevation and comic dismay or bitter grief, that make the best of Hafiz' monologues *dramatic actions,* unpredictably in motion. We read a Keats ode in exactly this way, or a section of Tennyson's "In Memoriam," or a Browning monologue—all are volatile, dramatic actions, often internally conflicted. Hafiz shows the same complexity as these poets in a comparable *art of process.*

The drama of Hafizian soliloquies can be almost unbelievably exciting. Giving a public recitation of poem 84 ("Bring me, taverner, the vine-juice"), even in an abridged form, at an academic conference (Bidney, 2009) was one of the most enjoyable activities I ever attempted. The poem is the longest Hafiz wrote (if he did indeed write it—the text is absent from Wohlleben's philologically critical edition, and we recall the contentious problem of canonicity). When you read the whole of this delightful piece aloud, you will find your voice getting gradually more resonant as you slowly rise out of your chair. The nearest parallel may be the "Song to David" by Christopher Smart (1722–1771), which affects me in the same way. The most thrilling part of Hafiz' oration comes when the inebriated speaker decides he is ready to "[l]eave behind the six-doored dwelling" (our world, with its directions of east, west, north, south, up, and down) and to escape "the old nine-headed serpent" (the world of the sky, with its nine spheres), for "All but God is vain and idle." After reading this poem, it was perhaps inevitable that Goethe would want to include a "Book of the Cupbearer" as one of the twelve parts of his own German-Persian lyric-epic. And after reading Hafiz' entire collection in Hammer's rendering, it was equally natural for Goethe to cultivate lightness, volatility, and subtle wit in *West-East Divan* while always trying out, of course, his own experimental meters.

The first lyric monologue in the present book helpfully sets the pattern for all the others, which may be considered as dramatic actions, poems of process. It is always printed first in all the widely varying versions of Hafiz' *Divan,* and a careful look at it may be the best way to gain an initial glimpse of him at work, for the poem has the qualities of an emblem or epitome of the whole. Characteristically, it is written in one of the effectively speakable strophes that Hammer invented. Following a frequent practice of Hammer himself, I offer a scansion diagram, a guide to the formal structure, with "x" meaning a weak syllable and "/" meaning a strong one. When I write

/xx /x x/
/xx /x x/
/x x/x /x
x/x /x /x /x

this will mean, for the reader who is reciting the poem aloud (as should always be done),

STRONG weak weak, STRONG weak, weak STRONG,
STRONG weak weak, STRONG weak, weak STRONG,
STRONG weak, weak STRONG weak, STRONG weak,
weak STRONG weak, STRONG weak, STRONG weak,
  STRONG weak.

Or you could think of it this way:

ONE and a TWO and a THREE,
ONE and a TWO and a THREE,
ONE and a TWO and THREE and,
and ONE and TWO and THREE and FOUR and.

To enjoy the poem as a Hafiz hearer, you need to keep the scansion pattern clearly in mind and emphasize it while reciting. I use apostrophes in words such as "ev'n" and "stol'n" to show that they each count as a word of only one syllable in the scansion; hints of this kind help you pronounce the words in the way best suited to strengthen that pattern. A Hafiz poem is a script for actors.

A few more words about form will offer help to the new hearer before we look at Hafiz' first Divan lyric. A Hafiz poem is not only a script for actors but a score for music lovers. In the way that choral librettists do, I write "heav'n," and "sev'n" when I want the word read as one syllable: you will be familiar with this if you like to hear or sing Handel's "Messiah." When rhythmic clarity is needed, a syllable is marked to show where a beat falls. I write not "Hafiz" but "Háfiz," to make it clear that, like Hammer and Goethe, I pronounce the name with a stress on the first syllable, HA-fiz, when I am translating his poetry. I put a stress mark when writing "Hécuba," "Hýades," "réspite," the verb "frequént," and a few other words, because at times I hear them pronounced in ways that would not be right for the rhythm. Hyphenation is yet another way to clarify rhythm. Instead of "rose garden," I write "rose-garden" when I want the phrase to be heard as "STRONG weak weak," or "ONE and a." In special cases, writing two words as one can be an additional rhythmic aid: I write "beggarman" and "beggarmen" (thinking here of the wonderful Irish ballad "The Little Beggarman") so you will be sure to hear "ONE and a," "STRONG weak weak." "Cannot" is "STRONG weak," while "can not" is "weak STRONG."

Rhythm matters greatly, because you will be reading and hearing a book of word music. Rather than "speed reading," it calls for slow reading. If you do not want to read every poem aloud, then simply listen to an inner voice that recites them audibly as your eyes travel along the page. I often move my lips while reading lyrics, and I know that even when taking them in "silently," I cannot help moving facial muscles so long as I am hearing the virtual voice. Every poem in this book is a lyric in the root sense, word music you could sing as if accompanied on a lyre. The poet takes pride in a limpid line of dulcet tones: in poem 81, we are told that Hafiz' "melody charms are extensively known and well valued / From China to the Grecian fields." In "Englishing" him, I try to muster whatever skill I have acquired as violinist and fiddler, folksinger and choir member. The Hafizian lyric forms we enjoy in the Hammer re-hearings are not a "dead language" of expression—they are alive today, ready to be used this moment, every moment. That is why, whenever I encounter a form of ingeniously intricate and appealing beauty, as in poems 64 and 68, I write several verse "replies" to show how practical and tempting the strophe is, no matter how different it may be from what we generally encounter nowadays. The trickier the lyric medium may seem, the more it cries out, "Try me!"

The opening strophe sets the free-floating mood and tone, as a request tendered to the cupbearer leads without transition to thoughts of love, something the young man knows plenty about:

> Give me the goblet, my boy,
> Hand it around to the guests:
> Love at the start—so easy,
> But then the difficulties follow.

Hammer has not tried to duplicate any of the original rhymes, but he is good at assonantal and alliterative patterns, and throughout this book I, too, have tried to shape these with care so the conversation will sound natural yet feel more melodious than the usual tavern talk.

> Came the aroma of musk
> Robbed from the curls of your hair,

Stol'n by the smiling East-wind:
With how much pain the heart flows over!

The East-wind is a major actor in the Hafizian world, for it bears the love-arousing, musky fragrance of the beloved's hair. But love is painful now, for departure is near, and the wagon driver beckons:

Hark to the innkeeper-mage:
Color the carpet with wine.
Travelers know the roadways;
Acquainted, they, with posting stations.

"The old mage," writes Wohlleben, "is in Hafiz' world picture a spiritual instructor, a so-called *morshed.*" He further explains: "The old mage, the pilgrim, the road, the stations, all these indicators point to the teachings of the mystics. To soil the prayer rug with wine is naturally a conscious act of sacrilege" (2004, 47–48).

Here the rich incongruities may be savored: Shakespeare would have loved them. Yes, a pilgrimage of a sort is promised, but first the poet defiles the prayer rug, heeding his spiritual instructor, the taverner. Mystical progress is a possibility, he smilingly grants, but meanwhile, more pressingly, he needs to rush off, for rumors have been rife regarding some questionable conduct.

How can I relish delight,
Ent'ring the tent of my dear?—
Calling me always, "Ready!"
Are bells: the caravan is leaving. . . .

Gloomy the shadow of night!
Whirlpool and wind of the sea—
How can you ev'n conceive them,
Who lightly on the banks are dwelling?

It all sounds quite brave, but perhaps the outrage of the locals at some of the behavior of the "monks," rather than merely a spiritual challenge, has made it necessary to confront the wilds of nature just at this point:

Yes, for well-gratified love,
I was a legend in town:

How can a thing stay hidden
When gossip flies abroad unhindered?

Háfiz, if peace you require,
Follow the valued advice:
Find your beloved; travel,
And leave the world, and never worry.

Says Wohlleben, "The mystical grounding of the poem is evident" (2004, 48). But we can equally claim that the ground is shaky, or, put otherwise, each bit of mystical territory given is at the same time spirited away. "Find your beloved": the Lord Almighty, or a new boyfriend in the next town? "Leave the world": the earthly, lower level of awareness, or merely the region where gossip about one's unmonkish conduct has become unbearable? "Never worry": because you will have found peace in the Lord, or because your reputation will not yet have had a chance to follow you?

The poem is touching but also unquestionably sly, in a whimsical way. The speaker starts by addressing the cupbearer and ends by talking mainly to himself, or to the reader, or to both. The religious metaphor of pious wandering is richened by the self-awareness of the sinner and yet compromised by the archness, the mischief of his wit. In Shakespeare's *Antony and Cleopatra,* the dissolute Antony redeems himself, in part, by just such a strength and complexity of imagination, building a poetic world out of his own fallibilities with the help of self-serving yet vaguely appealing transcendent imaginings as metamorphic as the shape of a cloud.

Hafiz, if a teacher, is a humble instructor. It is true that he likes to end a ghazal by praising himself, but only as a phrase turner in a well-made lyric. He rarely sets up as a moral model. I can think of only one poem where a note of righteous indignation enters ("Flee from the wrath of the Lord, lest He avenge the Qur'an!" at the end of poem 45), but even this warning arose from the desolation of unrequited love, and it may be thought to contain more than a hint of self-satire. Hafiz, the tavern amorist in wine-spotted cowl, is well aware of his many failings. We see this in the modest epitaph he includes in poem 34:

Turn not your footsteps away
From Háfiz' gravesite.
If he be sunken in sin,
He'll trust in heaven.

In poem 74, he is a fallen angel, bird of a higher sky, with the letter *alif*, "oneness" or friendship, still graven on his heart. The man is a charmer, not a preacher. That is why Ralph Waldo Emerson wrote, in his "Adradyn Nemontai Aiona" ("Not in tears but in joy do they possess life"),

> "A new commandment," archly said the Muse,
> "I give,—Thou shalt not preach, (my dismal one)!"
> Luther, Fox, Behmen, Swedenborg, grew pale,
> And held their speech; and rosier clouds upbore
> Hafiz & Shakespeare with their happy choirs.
> (ll. 10–14; *Poetry Notebooks* 103)

I could have developed these rather involved thoughts in my "Reply" to poem 1. Instead I only imply them, writing in a vein closer to the tradition of the Persian commentators and of Wohlleben's more edifying notes, offering a bemused little homily based loosely on Hafiz. Spurred by the wind-blown energy of his final lines, I end my poem in parallel fashion with joy in the prospect of mind-widening travel:

> Hope be a spur as we ride,
> Covered in cloud or in sun,
> Holy the rolling motion,
> And heartened by the breath of heaven.

My replies, I hope, will always be as unpredictable as Hafiz' poems. He is never boring to speak with or to hear. Hammer has helped bring this amazing man alive. Offering a word of caution, Wohlleben warns the reader:

> One may point out that Hammer's errors obviously did not hinder Goethe in discovering a "true" Hafiz in his text. That is correct, but it is a special case ("Sonderfall"). In the last analysis, we cannot expect that every German reader of the Hammer text be capable of the same hermeneutic intuition and divination as our great poet. (2004, 15)

Having accepted this challenge, I now can only hope the reader of the text that follows may be willing to consider my work another "special case." As we wander along the roads and past the posting stations, may you find enough intuition and divination to make you want to travel farther.

A Note on the Formatting of Poems

Since the Hammer-Hafiz *Divan* is an experiment in applying a wide range of rhythmic patterns in lyrics, I have carried over the experimental mentality in my formatting of the poems, using a variety of devices for contrasting effects. As a general rule, the greater the indentation of a line, the fewer syllables or beats it has. The traditional way to print an elegiac distich (see e.g., poem 6) is to indent the second line of each couplet, because it has fewer syllables. In poem 2, the three-beat, even-numbered lines are indented and the four-beat, odd-numbered ones are not, so the visual and aural contrasts are mutually reinforcing. Poem 64 and its "replies" embody the most intricate rhythm scheme found anywhere in the book, and here, indentations of varied lengths will give your eye a helpful road map of the unusual rhythms you will hear.

Another general rule is that lyrics in which the lines have rhythm units ("feet") of varied lengths are less likely to contain indentations. Here, I have judged that the changes between two- and three-syllable rhythm units within a line or between lines are just as important to hear as are the changing numbers of beats per line. Keeping track of all this may involve some complexity for the unaccustomed ear, so I want in these cases to keep the formatting simple.

An exception to this second rule is poem 66, written in the startlingly lively classical rhythm pattern called "alcaic." Here, line 4 in every stanza (or "strophe," a synonym you will often hear) is indented because it has fewer beats than lines 1 and 2, and line 4 is, in addition, doubly indented to show how dramatically unusual its rhythm is. Alcaic poems are often formatted this way, as, for example, in the works of Friedrich Hölderlin, who loved the ancient form. The strophes look like birds migrating in formation.

Poems of

Wine and Tavern Romance

1. HÁFIZ-HAMMER I.1–2 ELIF 1: ELA JA EJUHES—SAKI EDIR KASEN VE NAVILHA

/xx /x x/
/xx /x x/
/x x/x /x
x/x /x /x /x

Give me the goblet, my boy,
Hand it around to the guests:
Love at the start—so easy,
But then the difficulties follow.

Came the aroma of musk
Robbed from the curls of your hair,
Stol'n by the smiling East-wind:
With how much pain the heart flows over!

Hark to the innkeeper-mage:
Color the carpet with wine.
Travelers know the roadways;
Acquainted, they, with posting stations.

How can I relish delight,
Ent'ring the tent of my dear?—
Calling me always, "Ready!"
Are bells: the caravan is leaving. . . .

Gloomy the shadow of night!
Whirlpool and wind of the sea—
How can you ev'n conceive them,
Who lightly on the banks are dwelling?

Yes, for well-gratified love,
I was a legend in town:
How can a thing stay hidden
When gossip flies abroad unhindered?

Háfiz, if peace you require,
Follow the valued advice:
Find your beloved; travel,
And leave the world, and never worry.

Reply

Here at the start of our trip,
All of the themes are in place:
Lover becomes a pilgrim
When even drink proves unavailing.

Roadway and station and stops,
Mystic the lore of the mage—
Traveling, for a Sufi,
Alone may grant a happy answer.

Now the procession will halt,
Briefly be given to thought—
Starting again, determined
The outward bound to seek unyielding.

Then, should the energy flag,
Spirit be falling asleep,
Caravan bells on camels
The wander-group will, warding, waken.

Many may fail, and their goal
Seem but a guttering flame. . . .
Never surrender, goaded
By duty on the heart incumbent.

Six are the days of the week
Lent for the mercy, the search:
Seventh arrives, and shining,
We pray, will be the bliss awaited.

Hope be a spur as we ride
Covered in cloud or in sun;
Holy the rolling motion,
And heartened by the breath of heaven.

2. HÁFIZ-HAMMER I.3–4 ELIF 2:
EI FURUGHĬ MAHĬ HUSN ES RUĬ RACHSCHANĬ SCHUMA

x/ x/ x/ x/
x/ x/ x/x

The moon of beauty borrowed light
Your brilliant face emitted;
It radiated gleams of grace—
Your chin's attractive dimple.

The thoughts that I would shape, collect—
How might I well unite them
With locks of your resplendent hair
So tousled and disheveled?

My spirit, as when dying, rose
Up to my lips to see you:
Shall it escape? Or go back down?
Declare your lordly pleasure!

Should you pass by, lift up my cloak
Now dusty all and bloody,
For many sacrificed to you
Are fall'n upon this roadway.

My heart is orphaned. O, proclaim
To friends the grievous tiding!
With you, O friends, my spirit cries
In fellowship of sorrow.

What good is self-restraint to one
Who has beheld your glances?
The light upon your countenance
Was for his eye a lightning.

Let East-wind bring me a bouquet
From cheeks, of roses, ruddy,
Perhaps aroma to convey
With pollen of his gardens.

May you live long, and may your wish
Be ever granted, inn boys!
Although my glass, when I was there,
Was never full, I'll say it.

Then listen! Háfiz now will pray.
And say amen, he's praying:
Give me this day my daily bread
From—sweet!—the lips of friendship.

O Morning-wind, depart for Yazd!
And tell the local people:
The head of any ingrate will
Deserve your polo mallet.

Though I from you am distant far,
My spirit yet is nearer:
For I'm the servant of your shah
And glad to laud your merit.

I'm heartened, and I beg the Lord
You, king of kings, may help me!
I kiss the ground before your tent,
The vault of Háfiz' heaven.

Reply

A torn-out page of daily life
With maelstrom-changed emotion:
Despair, entreaty, prayer, hope,
Then grateful, riddling homage.

The Shíraz friend, the shah of Yazd—
They have no clear connection.
And none can tell what justified
The sudden shift in focus.

The friend—a king implored in vain
Who yet requires allegiance?
A rebel seems in conflict here
With such a humble subject!

And yet the clear-obscure appeals—
    Each thought or mood a current
Upborne by swift and riddling wind
    Upon a stormy crossroads.

3. HÁFIZ-HAMMER I.5–6 ELIF 3: SAKI BENURĬ BADE BER EFRUS DSCHAMI MA

/x /xx /x /x /x

Tavern keeper, with wine the goblet lighten;
Chanter, sing, for our deepest wish is granted;
I perceive, in the glass, loved cheeks' reflection.
Listen, you that have felt no joy in drinking:
Drunken frenzy befits the eyes of comrades;
Drinking boldly removes the reins and bridle.
I will favor the handsome men, but only
Till the slenderer cypress-man approaches.
He whose tongue is ensouled by love's immortal:
In the Book of the World I'm famed forever.
I am fearful that, come the Day of Judgment,
Wine and "bread of the wise" will not prove equal.
East-wind, passing the rose grove in your travel,
Send a word to my dear one from his comrade.
You, ethereal flood, and you, O moon boat,
Sink unseen in the ocean of his kindness.
Scatter eagerly, eye, the seed of teardrops:
I would catch in my net the bird of pleasure.

Reply

Steady tread, with a risky leap of daring:
Dactyl, faster, amid the plodding trochees.
Here's a man who confronts the Day of Judgment
Not with fear, but a loving speculation:
Wine is better than all the pious offer.
Who's the judge that would grant the novel thesis?
One magnanimous, big in mind, with spirit
Wider spread than the very heav'n above us,
Where the moon, little viewed, would sink forever,
Tells of pleasure to kindred wine-believers.
We that hunt for a sermon allegoric
Baffled halt for a moment—never longer!
Joy and love in their wider acceptation
Blend, for us, with a higher bliss abounding.
Don't forget: when a lyric gift is added,

Which the Book of the World enriches, lending
Immortality of the tongue well-honeyed,
Glory-ways are complete, the soul in Eden.

4. HÁFIZ-HAMMER I.7–8 ELIF 4: SOFI BIA KI ÁJNE SAFEST DSCHAMRA

/xx /xx /xx /xx /xx /x—
    /xx /xx /xx /x

Sufi, come here! and look down in the mirroring depth of the goblet—
    Pleasure behold of the wine, of its purple!
Looking for hidden significance, ask of the adepts of drinking—
    High-ranking Sufis have never attained it.
No one has caught the Simúrg, so your trap you had better cast farther—
    Swelling the net are but winds of the morning.
Up! make the most of the day; even Adam our father, in Eden,
    Couldn't get wine any longer when fallen.
Knock back a couple of cups at the feast of our life, and then onward!
    Seek not a steady delight under heaven.
Youth went away, O my heart! and the flowers unplucked and unsampled—
    Virtue, repute, you must covet when aging.
East-wind, awake! for a faithful disciple of drinking is Háfiz—
    Greetings convey to the lord of the tavern.

Reply

Anka, Simúrg are the names of the bird-king who since the beginning
    Hour of the world has endured unbeholden.
Solomon had him in service for taming the jinns while they labored—
    Then to the mountain of Kaf he retreated,
There to partake of a tranquil philosopher-peace unremitting,
    Ever transcendent, a cloud-rounded summit.
Seek in a goblet simurgal a wisdom eluding the Sufi—
    Emblemed, a mystery. Fleeting contentment!
Wines of the Highest are only prepared for the righteous in Eden—
    Duty and work are required of the servant.
Háfiz might want to impress on the mind the enlightening moral;
    Yet his two-minded crepuscular vision
Militates here, as throughout the perceptive collection, against it:
    Dawning is winelike, of rubious color.

5. HÁFIZ-HAMMER I.8–9 ELIF 5: SA KIA BERCHIS VE DERDICH DSCHAMRA

/x x/ x/x x/
x/x x/x x/

Taverner, up, and hand me the glass,
        And bury the worries in wine!
Give me the glass, and pour me the drink,
        Away with the wearisome cowl!
Bad will it sound to wise-guided minds,
        But why be concerned with repute?
Bring me the cup! The rest we'll forget—
        A waste of our fugitive time.
Smoke from the glow aflame in the breast
        Has molten the cold folks away.
Heart of a fool! In people I find
        Not one to be trusted like you.
Surely no comfort's needed by me,
        For everything vanished at once!
Háfiz, be patient, early and late;
        That all may turn out as you wish.

Reply

Blue was the shade a Sufi would wear
        When scolding our poet in scorn.
Goethe would later loudly complain
        That cowl-wearing critics were harsh:
Color might change, but habit would *not*—
        With rebel opinion it clashed.
Háfiz regretted, many a time,
        The Sufi-adherent constraint—
Yet, as the bard belonged to the group
        That followed the leader Hassán,
They would exhort him, like it or not,
        The rule of the order to guard.
Sufi charisma blossomed in love—
        And morals, the afterthought, stung.

6. HÁFIZ-HAMMER I.9–11 ELIF 6: DIL MEREVED SI DESTEM SAHIBI DILAN MODARA

/xx /xx /xx /xx /xx /x
/xx /xx / – /xx /xx /

Out of my hand flew my heart, O you folk that have heart in abundance!
Woe, by the Lord, is my fate! Now is the mystery fled!
Yesterday Nightingale sang of the rose and the wine, and so purely—
Bring me the wine of the morn, sleepyhead drunkard, at once!
Look in the goblet, the miracle-mirror of great Alexander:
There you'll be spying on plans wily Daríus had laid.
Grace-bearing Master, accept all my thanks for the blooming well-being;
Ask how your dervish may feel, also, if leisure you have.
Here and beyond, our tranquillity rises from heeding two mottoes:
Friends magnanimity give, friendship dispense to a foe.
Entry I'm roughly refused to the land of the fine reputation—
Trifler, if you are denied, struggle to alter your lot!
Bitter the drink that a pious one labeled the mother of vices—
Lovelier-tasting to me, far, than a virginal kiss:
Times are unfriendly? Well, here is a friend, an arousal to relish!
Alchemist, beggar it turns richer than Egypt's Karún.
Never be stubborn: your candle-flame glowing will gutter, extinguished,
Rock turning wax in one's hand, whom the fond lover would please.
Beauties of Persia with language well-honeyed new energy lend you.
Taverner, give the good news—quick!—to the pious and old.
Ah, it's not willingly Háfiz a garment had soiled from the goblet;
Shah, who in splendor are dressed, pardon your servant the flaw.

Reply

Now I'm beginning to see why our Emerson valued the poet
Háfiz so greatly he claimed Shakespeare and he were at one:
Loved for reluctance to preach, they are paired in the Emerson heaven:
Shining the choirs who commence, viewing their entry on high.
Hear but the verses I've rendered—they're motley, disordered, peculiar,
Humanly varied and strange, wise and eccentric, alive!
Lover and sinner and drinker and beggar and singer, implorer,
Learnéd in legend and lore, pouring a life into lines
Destined for centuries—ever-refreshing, the pulse of the moment.
Memories come into mind, Will, of how many a play!

Falstaff and Henry, and how many yearners, and how many doubters!
    Jester and monarch and more. Pen-wielding, spear-shaking twain!
Apt-emblematic the wine-mark—so maculate, labile the speaker;
    Penitent, rebel entwined—hapless and witty entwinned.
Rumi in rising became overpowered by mystical brightness;
    I, in imagining, brought comic Nasreddin to aid
Balance in thought, as a man that some humor can add to the brilliant
    Air getting thin on the height—warmer the "fool" that we need.
Háfiz I like for complexity—tragedy, humor combining:
    Here is a toast: may you rule seven more centuries! Hail!
Emerson knew he had gained irreplaceably from your acquaintance:
    Credit to him as to you—fellow delighters in life.

7. HÁFIZ-HAMMER I.11–12 ELIF 7: PREWNAKI AHDI SCHEBAB EST DIGER BISTANZA

x/ x/ x/ x/ x/x
x/ x/ x/ x/ x/x

The gardens, fresh in youthful grace, are blooming,
        And Rose gave Nightingale a gladsome tiding.
O Morning Wind, to meadows young you're coming,
        I hail the rose, the basil, and the cypress!
When he caresses me, the kindly cupboy,
        With eyelash-broom I'd gladly sweep the threshold.
You play at polo-ball with amber mallet—
        I'm hit! you needn't strike me any harder.
I fear that those who mock the steady drinker
        Will lose their own belief within the tavern.
To be God's friend to men will mean resistance
        Like Noah's to the overwhelming flood-tide.
What good's a palace towering to heaven
        To one who shortly in the dust will slumber?
O Canaan's Moon! May yours be throne of Egypt:
        It's time you, Joseph, left your gloomy prison.
Desire no bread, but leave the worldly hostel!
        The earthly publican each guest will murder.
I don't know what you're doing with your hair-locks,
        It only made the musk aroma stronger.
Then, Háfiz, drink your wine!—enjoy the morning.
        Make *your* Qur'an no hypocritic mind trap.

Reply

A Joseph would be Háfiz, out of prison,
        A Noah who dismissed the flood—a droplet!
The surest means of evermore escaping
        The danger of a jail or threat of drowning,
Or fatal sentence, long incarceration
        Resulting from rejection by a lover
(In poetry not giv'n to understatement,
        For Háfiz would luxuriate in symbols
Equating him with heroes in the scripture),
        Would be to leave the inn of earth completely.

Did not the musk of hair remain enticing,
    Were not the wine (reprovable allurement)
A sweet alternative to sequestration
    Within the cold monastic walls' withdrawal,
He well might wish to flee the ark, the tavern,
    And, flying skyward, seek the very heaven.
The polo-game, the love-humiliation,
    The failure of the nightingale that's likely
(For though we seem to hear a hopeful tiding,
    We know that roses doom to disabusal)
Might drive a troubadour to desperation
    Were not the melody itself a comfort.

8. HÁFIZ-HAMMER I.13–15 ELIF 8: EGER AM TURKĬ SCHIRASI BEDEST ARED DILĬ MARA

/xx /xx /xx /xx /xx /x
    /xx /xx /xx /x.

I, if the youth from Shiráz took my heart in his hand, for his beauty-
    Mark would bestow Samarkand and Bokhara.
Taverner, hand me the wine, for in heaven you'd vainly be seeking
    Róknabad's flowery bank, or Mosella's.
Woe! for the rogues with enticing black eyes and with gestures endearing
    Rob all restraint from the heart, as the Turks do.
Love, when ungratified, doesn't require all the beauty my friend has—
    Faces alluring will need no adornment.
Stay with the poet, the goblet, and seek not the things that are hidden—
    No one has found them, and no one will find them.
Joseph's enravishing beauty explains the enchantment of loving:
    Love rent asunder the veil of Zuleika.
Heed my advice—be aware that a youth of a high, noble breeding
    Treasures the reverend words of an elder.
Ill have you spoken? Forgiven! 'Tis fitting the ill had been spoken;
    Bitter goes well with your lips and their sweetness.
Háfiz, you've lined up your melody gems; they're the beads on a necklace,
    Pleiad-like, worth a bestrewal in heaven.

Reply

(1)

Thrilling, the distich that opened a lyric where love spoke to power!
    Timur the Great didn't find it amusing.
Legend proclaims that he summoned the singer to court with a query:
    "What may it mean, your colossal presumption?
Dare you belittle the splendor of realms your omnipotent ruler
    Conquered in lightning-like triumph of battle?
You Samarkand and Bokhara would grant, and without hesitation,
    Both, for a beauty-mark? Better explain it."
Háfiz replied (in the version von Hammer presented and relished),
    "Sorry, my writing was badly reported.
Here's what an accurate transcript will show you I plainly had written:
    'Gladly I'd give, from Bokhara, two pastries.'"

Aptly he sprang from the trap with agility all have applauded—
        Many the ways they re-tell of the triumph.
Don't be surprised the temerity's loved, for a "fool" to Czar Ívan,
        As to King Lear, in a madness poetic
Spoke, with a boldness incomparable, to a monarch besotted:
        Touched by the God they were gifted, permitted.

(2) On Hammer's Praise of Háfiz, Elif 8
for Katharina Mommsen

Honored by princes, loved by friends,
Resting in bloomy-bowered garden,
To Háfiz learning pleasure lends,
Dewed-flower mercy, Allah's pardon.

Dynasties, moved to battle by
Mutual turbid hatred rose:
Laid waste in tow'ring flames would lie
All Asia from the striving foes.

The empires in their turn were doomed
To fall, and by the selfsame law:
When, at the last, grave Timur loomed,
The gazing nations quaked in awe.

The sovran welcomed Háfiz now
With grace, though in a lyric he
Wrote as a man who would not bow
Despite how great a king might be:

Bokhara, Samarkand, he claimed
(The main adornments of the realm),
Or other prize that might be named,
Were he to hold the empire's helm,

He would exchange, right gladly too,
For but one thing: the beauty-mark
That his Beloved let him view:
A simple word! Let rulers hark.

The more the rumbling thunders crashed,
Colliding kingdoms, rife with rage,

In riving brilliance lightnings flashed,
The sweet-serene Iranian sage

The more appeared both calm and wise:
Half-mystic, smiling in the night,
He sang of the unsleeping sighs
Of Nightingale for rose-delight.

Then let the horror of the storm
That would convulse the Orient
Roar on! Affinities that form
A stiller wisdom had been lent

To him who caroled Love and Wine:
Abounding chaos would but free
One dowered by this gift divine
Of inward-lighted liberty.

For had he waited till the time
Long-envied peace at length might come
We'd never hail that halidom
We feel in every healing rhyme.

Now therefore let us learn and long
The lesson cherish that we've heard:
Who sings of Wine and Love a song
Can make which like the holy word

Beyond the bound of mortal bane
May last, on lips to hover—ah!—
When lofty names of Tamerlane
And Jenghiz Khan and Nadirshah

Will only as a burning scar
Be known in mankind's memory:
A warning and a mark to mar.
So, rather, hark to Háfiz. He,

Made bold by morning-evening star,
Embroidered clear and lyric hymn
To Love and Wine, twinned lights that are
The eyes of choiring seraphim.

9. HÁFIZ-HAMMER I.16–17 ELIF 9: SAHA BELUTF BÜGU AN GHASELĬ RANARA.

/x /x /x /x

Say caressingly, O East-wind,
To the fleet gazelle, the slender:
Fevered love for you has driven
Me to mountains, to the wasteland.

Why does not the sugar merchant
(Life to him by God be granted)
Ask about the mood and feeling
Of the candy-wanting parrot?

When you're sitting with the dear one,
By his side the wine imbibing,
All the other friends remember
Wand'ring like the wind bewildered.

Rose, the pride does not beseem you
Which you flaunt in all your beauty,
So that haughtily you never
Of the nightingale take notice.

Only recommended measures
Help to capture the beloved,
Clever birds avoiding deftly
Fowler-trap or net well hidden.

Who will tell me why with features
Nobly shapen of the faces
Moonlit-bright, the eyes in darkness
Cannot lend me their attention?

In your beauty I discover
Not a flaw that's worth the naming,
Save, as in so many handsome,
Lack of faithfulness in loving.

For the boon of dear companions,
For the friendship-favor grateful,
Have regard that many, distant,
Over wilding heath are roaming.

What the wonder, then, in heaven
When, by Háfiz' song awakened,
To the mellow lute of Zohra
The Messiah's gladly dancing?

Reply

Pilgrim angels Hárut, Márut,
Clothed in garb of walking mortals,
Met the saintly woman Zohra
And attempted to seduce her.

They were punished, hanged in fetters
By their feet, a doom disgraceful,
Near a Babylonian fountain.
For reward the blameless lady

In the fourth of spheric heavens,
Would assume the form of Venus,
Playing on her lute forever,
Star of evening, soul of morning.

Planets roundelay are making
As enravished by her music
They the harmony are sounding
That on earth was rudely sundered.

In her sphere the prophet Jesus,
Named Messiah by Muhammad,
Joining gladly in the dancing
Pays the maiden-virtue homage.

How remarkable that Háfiz'
Love lament aroused the prophet,
Who a countervailing gladness
With the lady might awaken!

Holy, as a dance-companion,
Is the prophet to the poet:
Boon to both—poetic ardor
Lauding daily the Creation.

Nine the strophes of the singer,
Nine the lordly orbs of heaven,
Nine the Muses when the Grecians
Adumbrated later Eden.

I this hymn would fain not finish
Till I've praised the poet also
For compassionate remembrance
Of the friends in desert moaning.

10. HÁFIZ-HAMMER I.18–19 ELIF 10: DUSCH ES MESDSCHID SUI MECHANE AMED PRĬMA

/x /x /x /x

Yesterday our Sufi elder
Left the mosque to try the tavern.
O you pious men, inform me:
How should we direct our actions?
How can we, disciples faithful,
To the Kaaba turn our faces
When the sheikh who is our father
To the inn is gladly going?
Let's make common cause together
With the the genial tavern keeper!
In the Book of Fate it so was
Immemorially written.
See! a breeze, through hair-locks rushing,
All the world for me has darkened!
There's the sum of the advantage
That your tresses long have brought me.
When my heart at last had captured
Rest within its spirit-netting,
You unrolled your fragrant hair-locks,
And my prisoned prey had vanished.
If the intellect could fathom
How the hearts are caught in tresses,
Held, infatuate, in bondage
It would lose that understanding.
Of the fair Qur'an of Beauty
Was your face a revelation:
Therefore now my lines are breathing
With a beauty graceful, higher.
How could fiery sighs, the glowing
Of my breast in lover's ardor,
Through the night continue burning
With your stony heart immobile?
See: the arrow-sigh of Háfiz
Flown away into the heaven!
Have compassion for the sender—
And be fearful of my arrows.

Reply

It was thought by commentators
That the missiles of the thinking
In the hidden mystic vision
Couldn't rightly be commended
As the vehicles of entry
Meant to part the veil of heaven
For the novice uninstructed.
Be aware! Let not the reader
Claim the poet didn't tell him:
Sapientibus sufficit.

11. HÁFIZ-HAMMER I.19–21 ELIF 11: PE MULASIMANĬ SULTAN KI RESANED IN DŪARA

x/ x/ x/ x/
x/ x/ x/x

To Sultan's followers, who'll bring
My humble, poor petition?
Turn not your gaze away from him
Who, beggar, thanks your Lordship.
My rival had I fled, for he
Is but the Devil. Fleeing
To Mighty God, I hope He may
Consume that foe in flaming.
You set the very world on fire
When rays your face enlighten—
Explain, what might the reason be
Your rule is not far milder?
How lovely does the form appear
To him that loves the ruler!
The countenance, than moon more bright—
The stature of a cypress!
I spend the night in waking hope
That with the breath of morning
Might gladsome tiding come to me
Afresh from loving comrade.
And when with eyelash movement you
For bloodshed give the signal,
Consider who the rascals are
That wide astray might lead you.
My heart has lost the blood of life
Because your eyes enchant me.
And ah! my darling, have regard
How you have killed your servant!
When, Háfiz, in an exile-land
You feel your heart-life waning,
Await from him a joy renewed,
Restoring happy fortune.

Reply

The one who captured Háfiz' heart
Not only as a monarch
But even as a god is called
To end the separation.
Political-religious in
His amatory language,
The poet may a dirge convert
To fulsome panegyric.
Three kinds of rulership combine—
The strain continues growing
'Mid rapture of the servitude
In suppliant abasement.
How long before the war breaks out
In rebel fires arising?

12. HÁFIZ-HAMMER I.30–31 BER 1: GUSTEM IN SULTANI CHOBAN RAHM KUN BER IN GARIB

x/x x/ x/x
x/ x/ x/x
x/x x/x x/
x/ x/ x/x

I said to the King of Beauty,
"Have mercy on a stranger."
Reply: "He is out of his mind,
That crazy-headed stranger."

I answered him, "Stay, and hear me!"
He spoke: "I beg your pardon,
But how can the child of the house
Hear woe from such a stranger?

Who sleeps in a kingly chamber
And lies on ermine blanket
Knows naught of a pillow of rock,
The thorn-bed of a stranger."

"O You, in whose hair-enchainings
Full many comrades languish,
How finely that beautiful mark
Becomes you, nothing stranger—

The delicate hairs appearing
On silky skin yet stranger,
Though paintings from China are framed
Like this, and never stranger;

Your face in the light's revealing
The heady wine's reflection
As blossom of purple may boast
The hedge-rose, lovely stranger.

I said to the Night, 'Your hair is
Admired by every stranger.
It's fit that at dawn he laments
Your parting—grieving stranger.'

Your hair-crest—a blacker midnight;
My friend," I said, "no stranger
Need seem to you all of my pain,
The sorrow of a stranger."

Reply

I'll try to portray the feeling
Of writing something stranger
Than all that I ever was taught
And—what is even stranger—

The heightening life it lent me!—
As in the verse Olympics
The athlete of intricate form
Would feel. Don't think it stranger.

So, Háfiz, I'm rough but ready:
Whatever scheme you offer,
I'll risk it and see if I win!
Although I be a stranger

To some of what Persia valued
In medieval writing,
I grow when I travel, and so
I hope, a Sindbad-stranger,

A magical realm to relish
With jinn and angel flying
Wherever my port may invite.
Then let me be a stranger!

A bard who no longer wanders
Forsakes imagination,
Abandoning tamely his task.
What failure could be stranger?

To Rumi the world was flaming,
One energy, in motion—
The soul that in comfort would rest
A sullen life-estranger.

Of course we'll encounter trials
And be prepared for danger!
But effort empowers the heart
To dark dismay a stranger.

An oddity, though, arises:
The more the mind imagines
The less can identity thrive.
"I write." Who's "I"? A stranger.

Odyssean be our hero,
A Captain Nemo, No-One;
Unending horizon the home
Of *Un-self*—nothing stranger!

13. HÁFIZ-HAMMER I.31–32 BER 2: MIDENUD SUTHVE KELLE BEST SAHEB

x/x x/x
x/x x/
x/ x/ x/x

The morning is smiling
And cloudlets approach:
Some wine! some wine! you comrades!

The cheeks of the tulips
Reflecting the dew:
Some drink! some drink! you comrades!

The meadow is wafting
A paradise breath;
Bring purest wine—don't hide it!

The rose takes her seat on
The emerald throne:
Bring tribute—flaming rubies!

But locked is the tavern—
How tiring!—again:
The doors—pray let them open!

With springtime's arrival,
How odd it would seem
To keep the tavern shuttered!

To juice of the ruby
The lips have a right:
Appease our thirsting fever!

But, Háfiz, keep steady—
Feel never aggrieved:
Revealed will be your fortune.

Reply

I pray for the gift an
Impatience of mood
To shape into a chantey.

How many have waited
For someone to move
In lines of busy traffic

But never invented
A rhythm to sing
Away the hypertension!

14. HÁFIZ-HAMMER I.33–34 BER 3: SUBHĬ DEVLET MIDEMID GÙ DSCHAM HAMTSCHUN AFITAB.

/xx /xx /xx /xx /xx /x
/x x/ x/x x/x

Morning is laughing! Instead of the sunlight, just hand me the goblet!
Now is the time! The wine, let us have it!
Tavern—so still! But the innkeeper's friendly, the singer encouraged!
Day of spring air, the goblet, our youth-time!
Cheer up the spirit: elixir! The feast-day adorn with more beauty:
Add to the gold what's molten—the rubies!
Poet and darling extending a hand while the drunk ones are dancing:
Cupboy-caress—and drinkers awaken!
We are alone, and secure in the circle of intimate friendship—
Open are only doorways of pleasure.
Artfully nature has hidden the skill-giving grace of the wine-grape,
Rosewater secrets hid in the leaf-cup.
Ever since high on the Moon my ghazals have acquired an admirer
Zohra can hear the comforting lute-strum.

Reply

Rulers in Persia would drink to the sun of the springtime and bless it,
Holding the goblet Jémshid made famous.
So have we learned from the wonderful comment of Joseph von Hammer;
Then he provides a verse in a footnote:

Whoever sees the onyx-colored wine
Would think it onyx, by the heightened shine.
The two are truly jewels, rich and fine.

The liquid, solid both before me stand.
The former who may touch will stain his hand.
Should he but taste it—ah! the head feels grand!

Hammer, I never can thank you enough; with your music and learning—
Háfiz you place in Persia: I view him!
Daily I mentally drink to your health—may a houri in heaven
Festival wine decant at your table!

Zohra, the fair morning star, in the fourth of the spheres, hearing Háfiz,
Played on the lute her anthem for Hammer.
More: let me hope that the spirit of Jémshid, with goblet of ruby,
Lauding her, called: A toast to the poet!

15. HÁFIZ-HAMMER I.40–41 TA 1: PE DSCHAMĬ CHODSCHA VE HAKKĬ VE ADĬ DURUST

/xx /xx /xx /xx /xx /x
/xx /xx / – /xx /xx /

Aye, by the life of the master, the law of the ancients, the contract,
Ever your welfare shall be, daily, my prayer at dawn.
Truly my tears are outpoured as the flood over patriarch Noah,
Yet will your form in my heart never be taken away.
Ev'n if your parting had shattered my heart, still in myriad fragments
More is it worth than the hearts others may show that are whole.
Scold me no more for my drunkenness. Truly the guide to my loving
Fated me ages ago, his the eternal decree.
Candid remain, for the sun when arising if upright is clearer—
Slanted, the twilight betrays, blackness and shade interblent.
Never surrender, my spirit, your hope for the grace of the comrade—
Having made much of your love, better not trust in the mind.
Out to the wilds of the waste and the mountains I'm driven by madness—
Ah, what a burden, a chain—not to be lightened by you!
Asaph was mocked by the ant, and how rightly the creature rebuked him:
Solomon's ring had he lost—barely attempted to find!
Háfiz, don't grieve! From the thief of a heart don't demand compensation—
Is it the fault of the field when there's no growth in the tree?

Reply

Hammer would Háfiz compare to the bard of urbanity, Horace.
Yet in the lines we have read, wan, elegiac, distraught,
Surely a truer analogy lies in bold Ovid's *Amores.*
Listen awhile to the famed Elegy One of Book Two:
"Brave—my intention to chant of the Battles of Heaven, to sing of
Hundred-armed Gyges, and well I had prepared for the task.
I was about to begin with the vengeance of Tellus, with Ossa
Fall'n from Olympus by dread Pelion crushed to his death.
I in my hands held the cloud, and His thunderbolt Jupiter surely
Might have been tempted to use, viewing a threat to the realm.
Ah, but my mistress, the cold one, in wrath, had her door slammed against me!
Jupiter, lightnings, I dropped. Banished, the god—he was gone.
Monarch, I'm asking your pardon; your thunder no longer could threaten
One who more deeply was moved seeing a door had been shut."

16. HÁFIZ-HAMMER I.41–43 TA 2: REVAKĬ MANSARĬ TSCHESCHMI MEN ASCHIANCĬ TUST.

x/ x/ x/x
x/ x/ x/ x/

My eyes, like tents, are ready;
To welcome and to shelter you.
Descend, come in, be gracious,
And let my dwelling be your home.
That beauty-mark and beard-down
Have robbed the hearts of ev'n the wise—
In wonder-working manner
They serve instead of net and bait.
In rose-endowed enjoyment
Delight yourself, O nightingale!
For with a lover's mourning
Alone you fill the meadow wide.
Let be to lips entrusted
The healing of my wounded heart:
The rubies, with their virtues,
Are kept within your treasury.
I'll never have the standing
To let me be quite near to you,
And yet you see my spirit
Come nearer, as your threshold-dust.
I do not spend on any
Beloved thing my gold of soul—
Your seal and signet only
Impressed, that I may cherish them.
My kind, chivalric rider,
The rarest art have you acquired—
To mount the horse of heaven
And tame it, willing, with your whip!
And how shall I, enamored,
Your thousand arts be countering,
The clever conjuration
Whereby you lead astray the skies!
The very spheres are dancing
Within the round of harmony
To which the tune's provided
By Háfiz' finest book of hymns.

Reply

Capricious lover-whimsy
Appearing as a pow'r that might
Be sovran of the heaven!—
To ride the mettled weather-horse
And wizard-like emboldened
To prove his magic mastery,
To show the heaven colder,
Then heated, as the feeling moves,
To cleave the sky with lightning—
Then, mild, a smile, with shining eye!
We note a quick transition
From lover-will when exercised
In unpredicted mood-swing
To mythifying pictures of
A strength to rule the heaven,
An arbitrary deity,
Whose verve the more was worshiped
The less it proved conformable
To humbled minds of mortals,
Confined by helpless intellect.
Did Horace, on occasion,
Conceive his Lálagē in terms
Of wit-transcending godhead
That, often kind, might yet invoke
A tempest unawaited?
In these, the honeyed lines he wrote,
I think I see a blending
Of Jove and the beloved maid:

> *Put me in wretched clime where barren northlands*
> *Never contain a tree with summer leafage,*
> *Land of a louring storm cloud—where a sullen*
> *Jupiter glowers:*
>
> *Ev'n as I lay where Phoebus' flaming chariot*
> *Scorches the land bereft of habitation,*
> *I would love Lálagē the sweetly laughing,*
> *Sweetlier speaking.*

17. HÁFIZ-HAMMER I.44–45 TA 4: SER IRADATI MAVE ASITANI HASUTI DOST

x/ x/ x/ x/
x/ x/ x/x

My head and will have made their way
To my beloved's threshold—
What's going on above my head
Is by her will engendered.
I never saw the likes of her
Although I held a mirror
To first the moon, and then the sun,
In hope to find a likeness.
What can the East-wind tell about
A heart-love's humble torment?
It's all entwisted, leaf in leaf,
As in a rose a-budding.
In all this evil, drunken world
I'm not the only drinker—
A head at times you'll find that's formed
Of clay as mug or tankard.
You must have used an amber comb
And drawn it through your tresses:
The West-wind—bearing fragrance, from
The earth, of musk and amber!
The petals of a meadow-rose
Are like your face in fragrance;
The cypress on the riverbank,
Meek rival of your stature!
Struck dumb, the art of eloquence
That might describe my longing—
How can it aid, that writing quill?
It's cracked, and vainly chatters.
Your face had entered in my heart—
A wish-fulfillment promise,
For good things ever follow when
We're well prepared to get them. . . .
It's not just now that Háfiz' heart
Upwelled in flames of passion;
His face—burned from eternity
And branded, as a tulip.

Reply

Two kinds of destiny with metaphor
Are lighted, as by sun through open door:
That of a pitcher made of potter's clay;
That of a tulip branded evermore.

Omar Khayyám, we know, had much to say
About the pots that the Creator may
Have fashioned as a worthy craftsman might,
But which from excellence have fall'n away.

We're fallible, and often only slight
Advance we daily make in doing right;
Our nature—predetermined, aye, in part—
But doesn't love our weakness try to fight?

For we are more than passive. In the heart
I feel the stir of action hourly start
With energy that can reveal desire!
No matter how our passion-pain may smart,

It's yet the center of the soul, a fire
That powers me to write, and Háfiz' lyre
To sound to Zohra in the higher sphere!
We're more than clay—we're rising from the mire.

What means the branding of the tulip here?
Sign, signet, and a seal, the marks appear
Of burning, of the ardor that we are:
And though there will be wounding woe, to sear

The spirit, carmine tulip hue to mar
With black as with a blemish, or a scar
Of passion past, love links me to the far
Aspiring, yearning life in whirling star.

18. HÁFIZ-HAMMER I.46–47 TA 5: AN SIEH TSCHERDE KI SCHIRINII AALEM BA OST

/x /xx /
/x /x /
/x /x /x /x
/xx /xx /

See the swarthy one? Look:
He the world made sweet.
Glowing eyes, the lips are laughing—
He will make happy your heart.

Honey-lipped, to be sure,
Worldly lordlings are.
Ah, but Solomon—it's *he* that
Carried the love-ring ensealed.

That's the beauty-mark, black,
There on lighter cheek,
Teaching me a single wheat-grain
Adam betrayed, and it's here.

Sages he will respect,
Friends he helps with God!
Where's the aid for broken hearts, then?
No one but he has the cure.

His the handsomest face,
Pure and virtue-bright,
Shining minds of both our world-realms
Wanting to walk at his side.

Ah, but whom can I tell?
Murderer, he smote
One who loved him, even though his
Breath, like Messiah's, may heal!

Number Háfiz among
Souls devoted. Why?
Spirits of the blesséd wander,
Him to accompany, friends.

Reply

Wheat-grain Adam betrayed!
Apples disregard.
They are mentioned not in Eden:
Time for a metaphor change.

19. HÁFIZ-HAMMER I.49–50 TA 7: AN SEHEBĬ KADRÌ KI GOJENDEHLĬ CHATVET IMSCHEBEST

x/ x/ x/ x/ x/
x/ x/ x/x
/x x/ x/ x/

The Night of Pow'r, of which the pious tell—
With starry fire—behold it!
Allah, what star has brought it back?

Amid that troop of riders how shall I
Like Solomon be riding,—
I, whom an ant had served as horse!

That none may ever touch, unmeriting,
His hair, the hearts are watchmen:
Everyone cries, "Give aid, O Lord!"

I faint before the dimple of his chin:
For myriad hearts are lying
Under that hollow in defeat.

The rider's mirror-holder is the Moon:
The sun below the hooves but
Dust underneath a battle-steed.

Behold the pale reflection on his cheeks:
The sun grows weaker, trembling,
Longing to share the brilliant light.

I can't from comrade's glass and ruby wine
Depart. For this, you pious—
My faith-confession—pardon grant!

Where drinks the raven of my writing-quill?
My Lord! his beak is dripping
From living waters' primal spring.

With eyelash-arrow he has made a wound
That ever tuneful Háfiz
With soul-empow'ring smile has healed.

Reply

I doubt the poet ever dared to print
A lyric more audacious:
Holy! the Night of Power when

Muhammad the Qur'an from God in Heav'n
Received and with the Angel
Struggled, and then with humbled will

Recited it aloud, that all might hear—
Awareness reawakened
Now by a Lover's heaven-ride!—

The horse he mounts recalling white Buraq,
The steed that through the spheric
Realms had the Prophet lordly borne.

Distinctions are negated: we behold
The Friend in pride resplendent
Gaze in the moon, a slave-held glass!

The chanter will admit that he proclaims
The creed of his religion:
Faith in a sky-triumphant Love

Who envy in the very Sun aroused
That looked on him and turned to
Dust underneath the lightning-steed.

The bard, who felt as if he rode an ant
Near Solomon in battle,
Here, with a pen by Eden filled,

Can write the scripture of his high belief,
A new Buraq be riding,
Singing a hymn—a Night of Pow'r!

20. HÁFIZ-HAMMER I.51–52 TA 8: METALEB TAAT VE PEIMAN VE SALAH ES MEN MEST

/x /x /x /x
/x /x /x /x

Don't require of me, the drinker,
Duteous conduct, deed of merit—
On the Day of Covenant to
Wine was I predestinated.

Since I had become accustomed
To attend the source of loving,
With a single word I uttered
Last farewell to all remaining.

Give me wine, that I may tell you
To what mystery I'm fated,
Whose the face to which I'm faithful,
What the fragrance I'm imbibing.

Mountains bear a lover's burden
Far less well than littlest emmet;
Drinker, never be despairing,
Waiting at the gate of mercy.

All except the eyed narcissus
(God from evil gaze defend it)
Have along the breadth of bluest
Heaven all their calm surrendered.

Gladly would I lend my spirit
To your lips to be their trophy—
In the fairest faces' garden
Never bud more bloomed in beauty.

Sadly, Háfiz now will mirror
Solomon—your love has done it;
I've a single royal pleasure:
Wind with empty hand I'm grasping!

Reply

Solomon, we learn from Hammer,
Triple treasure had been granted:
First, the magic ring that made him
Wisest of the world of spirits;

Then the wonder-glass wherein he
Learned what other kings were planning;
Finally, control of air that
For a wingéd mount would serve him.

Háfiz likes a bit of joking
Even if it's rather bitter—
Though I have no ring, he says, and
No prophetic wisdom-goblet,

In my hands the air I'm holding
May to Solomon's be likened—
Little good for transportation,
Yet an empty-helpful token

To remind me of the monarch
Who to love was ever faithful.
Wind is breath—at least I'm living,
If by weight of worry burdened.

Yet because the First Agreement
In the dawn before Creation,
When, in reverence together,
Human souls to God commended

All their trust, my fate had settled,
Link annealed to goblet-blisses,
Guilt awhile alleviating,
I can have some consolation.

21. HÁFIZ-HAMMER I.61–62 TA 13: BIA KI KASRĬ EMEL SACHT SUST BUNJADEST

/xx /xx /xx /xx /xx /x
/xx /xx / – /xx /xx /

Come! for the palace of hope will repose on ethereal columns:
  Come, and of course bringing wine—all of our life-days are wind.
Gladly, a slave, would I hallow my will to the spirit of courage,
  Happy all links to reject, bonds to the breadth of the world.
Now will I tell you how yesterday tidings of heavenly pleasure
  Hidden to others, to me newly a herald had brought.
O you high falcon in flight!—for the Tree of true Life is your dwelling—
  Our little corner of woe never could lend you a nest.
Upward!—they're summoning you from the summit, the peaks of the heavens—
  Baffled, I cannot divine why you remain in this net.
I'll be your guide and provide some advice—hearken well and then follow.
  Why? I have learned it from one who is a master indeed.
Faithfulness, truth never seek in the world of a frivolous woman—
  Myriad beaux had pursued *her*, the notorious bride.
Have no concern for the world—nor my helpful instruction abandon:
  Wisdom like this will confirm one who has given up whims.
Ruminate well on what happened before—clear your forehead of wrinkles:
  Neither to you nor to me comes what we might have desired.
Fickle, ephemeral ever, the likeable smiles of the roses:
  Well may the nightingale mourn—deep is the heart of our grief.
Why do you envy then, weakling, the streaming creations of Háfiz?
Welcome, he entered the heart—God-graced the phrase to be lent.

Reply

(I)

Joseph von Hammer averred that the lyric sublimity offered
  Here in a word of advice Persians yet treasure today.
Highest regard do they hold for the second two-liner, the distich—
  Great are the numbers, you'll find, saying it often by heart:
Gladly, a slave, would I hallow my heart to the spirit of courage,
  Happy all links to reject, bonds to the breadth of the world.
Háfiz, in general, people admire, and they relish repeating
  Verse at a holiday meal, love to interpret his thought.

Pleasant the banquet enhanced by reciting and allegorizing:
Who is the "maiden" deplored? What is the meaning of "wine"?
Háfiz, rejecting the lure of the world, and on pinion arising,
Bold, in the famous two lines, falconlike skyward to fly,
Holds allegoric attention: the bird—philosophic? Platonic?
Pious in leaving behind weakness, material mire?
True, the disgust had arisen from trouble with *one* worldly maiden
Rarely attending to plaints poured from a nightingale-throat—
Yet the contempt for what's lower invited a wide application,
Teaching you what to ignore, lordlier aim to attain.
Music that brightens the eye and enlightens the mind and the spirit
Gains even greater appeal once we an emblem discern
Helping the soul-bird ascend to a realm of ethereal hoping,
Rest from the snare and the net rounding one, careworn and gray—
Lending the breath of the poet the height of a loved aspiration
Arrowing cloud with an eye seeking the heavenly Sun.

(2)
FOR THOMAS OGGER

Yes! you are right, and we never will replicate moments that vanish,
Yet if the spirit remain, *this* we can daily invoke.
I am more distant than you from the great fourteenth-century Persian
(Oh, how I'd love to perceive all the "beyondness" you hear!)—
Yet I can offer the rhythm that Hammer, in rendering Háfiz,
Frequently liked to employ—bending, mellifluous tone.
Háfiz and Hammer were Gemini, fitted so well for each other!
(Beautiful emblem and bright: balance and friendship and calm.)
Turning the verse of the Persian to warm, conversational German,
Hammer a majesty found, writing of love and of wine,
Also of Eden and pilgrimage: all have *advanced to a grandeur.*
Liking the meter so well, why not employ it again,
Here, to convey, in my Hammer-Hafizian classical distichs,
What you have rendered for me? Let me attempt it right now!
Háfiz, you note, didn't write it, and yet it is perfectly suited,
Held in the depth of the soul, heavenly friendship to hymn:

Ah, what a stroke of good fortune when, after prolonged expectation,
One who had hoped could attain quickly the goal of his hope!
Nothing is finer, nor ever more fully rewarded than spirit,
Letting a breath that is lent speed from a friend to a friend.

22. HÁFIZ-HAMMER I.74–75 TA 20: BIREW BEKÎARÎ CHAD WAIS IN TSCHI FERJAD EST

/xx /xx /xx /xx /xx /x
/xx /xx / – /xx /xx /

Mind your own business, you preacher, don't trouble yourself with your shouting,
Truly my heart's in a whirl—what does it matter to you?
God, as from nothing, created a waist so uncommonly slender,
Here is the delicate point: how the small belt to unloose?
High in your realm will the beggarman never require the Eight Heavens!
He to your tresses enslaved wholly is free of the world.
I am disturbed, I admit it, distraught by the tumult of loving—
Yet perturbation has made all of my life blossom forth!
Do not complain then, my heart, the beloved's reluctance bemoaning—
When she acknowledges you, everything's proper and right.
Till I may paradise gain, playing flute on the lips of the lady,
All of the stir of the world seems, to my hearing, but wind.
Off, with your fairy-tale wishes and magical spell-conjuration!
Háfiz, be quiet—I've heard more than enough of such words.

Reply

Háfiz-and-Hammer, you write in the classical way with such freedom,
After I'm done there remain metrical rhythms in mind
Wanting to start on another creation of musical meaning,
Ruling my breathing and feet, moving the fingers to play.
Seven the hells, but the heavens are eight, for we know that the Sender
Meant that our Prophet should tell how to arise from a tomb—
Helped by the chant that like grasses and plants in a vernal returning
Offers a body of life, clothing the soul that was cold.
Yellow the sun in the heav'n like the ripest Iranian melon;
Red of our blood in the rose, Lote-tree in Eden of green—
Tender the soft russet-brown of the nightingale, lover despondent
Who in the blue of his flute bade what is lower goodbye.
Need we no magical amulet more than the meter of heartbeat:
Stretch out your arms to embrace—God!—and be taller than palm!

23. HÁFIZ-HAMMER I.75–77 TA 21: LALĬ SIRAB BECHUN TSCHNE LEBĬ JARĬ MEN EST

/x /x x/ x/x
/x /x x/
/x /x x/ x/x
/x x/

Reddest ruby, for blood a-thirsting,
Such the lips of my Friend!
These to view, and the soul surrender—
That is my fate.

Those who've known how the Friend can steal a
Heart, and chide me for this,
Let them be, by his eyes and lashes,
Blamed and disgraced.

Lead me, caravan guide, to somewhere
Else!—The gate of the town
Stands too near my beloved's dwelling—
Royalty-road.

I of Destiny am a servant—
Wanting steadiness, Love
Here a slave, and a drunken one, has
Tempted to love.

Spicy rosy aroma, and her
Chalice amber-infused
Are of fragrance the Comrade offered
Barely a breath.

Keep me not from the garden, watchman—
Grove where winds of the east
Loose the red-as-a-pomegranate,
Tear-streaming bloom.

Candies, water-of-rose elixir,
Healing lips of the Friend—
These the cure that the eye-narcissus
Kindly advised.

Know that Háfiz acquired the smoothness,
Honeyed-lovely, of song
Only from the speech of a tender
Friendly caress.

Reply

WITH GRATITUDE FOR THE NOTES OF JOACHIM WOHLLEBEN

Why, you wonder, the crimson ruby's
Thirsting, cruel, for blood?!
Gems, when cut, in their freshest redness
Used to be laid

(Then, they'd seem even more transparent,
Yet more carmine of hue)
Mid an animal's blood-filled liver
Warmly contained.

Why as red as the pomegranate
Seem the tears of the rose?
Heart-blood flow to the eyes, when rushing,
Colored them thus.

Much we learn from the commentator—
Fragrance, jewel, and bloom
Bring the dark of the heart-commandment
Into the day.

Mars and Venus are near-related—
Vainly Vulcan would try,
Forging fetters, to catch them—folly!
Not to be caught,

Blood-born, these are the Belle and Bellum,
Dawn and the End,
Rosy-fingered—and, yes, red-handed—
Fire in the sky!

24. HÁFIZ-HAMMER I.77–78 TA 22: RUSKIARIST KI SEWDAĬ BUTAN DINĬ MEN EST

/xx /xx /xx /xx /xx /x
/xx /xx / – /xx /xx /

Longing for beauty has been my belief and religion long-standing—
    That is a faith that can lend bliss to the woe-burdened mind.
Rightly to look at your ruby-mouth calls for the eye of the spirit—
    Distant, O far, far away! stands the mere eye of the earth!
Blest be my comrade! together we'll lend to the heaven adornment—
    You with your lunar-bright face, I with my pleiad-shine eyes
Ever since loving of you has a melody-eloquence taught me,
    I am the people's delight, lauded wherever I go.
Lend me yet longer benignly the poverty-gift of the spirit,
    Riches can merely deplete mind in its widening might:
Lord! What a pilgrim has viewed the great Kaaba of love's veneration
    Sought through a wasteland of thorns, turned to white jasmine entire!
How might your image be steered through the high-welling sea of my teardrops—
    Save by the Hýades taught, rain-constellation for eyes?
Háfiz, then chatter no more of the court of magnificent Párviz—
    Finer than Shírin by far, he whom my lyric would praise!

Reply

What may we write of the conflict dividing religion and beauty?
    Háfiz, you've granted a wide, bridge-making vision of life.
Face like a sun or a moon, and our eyes like the Pleiades gleaming—
    What does it mean but that we, blending the heaven and earth,
Spirit and body in one that, combining in viewing the beauty
    Fashioned for woman and man, filling with passion their eyes,
Come to the knowledge of One who was never "I am" till he made it—
    Never Creator could be, till he had deigned to create.
Favored as Maker, before He had anything made He was nameless.
    Making is Being for Him—ev'n as the two are but one
Also in Adam, in Eve, and in Adam and Eve come together.
    How might He be but in world, knowing Himself in that Form?
Beauty—six days in the making. The seeing of Beauty meant Sabbath.
    Viewing meant making as well. Singing will make even more.

25. HÁFIZ/HAMMER I.78 TA 23:
MENEM KI KOSCHEĬ MEICHANE CHANKAHĬ MENEST

/x /x /x /x x/
/x x/ /x /x /x

I'm the one who turned the pub to a mosque.
Innkeeper's word—early morning blessing.
Thrums the lute today no song of the morn?
Calm will I stay—chanting rue, regretful.
Cloister, pub—your joy alone do I want,
Let it suffice. Heaven is my witness!
Rather than a prince a beggar I'd be:
Torment from you—*there's* my fame and honor.
Sunlight I will relish: right at the gate—
There will my face wait for my beloved.
Death may tear apart the tent of my life—
Why should I move? Here are life and pleasure. . . .
Even when a sin has never been willed,
Better admit, Háfiz, when you're guilty.

Reply

Torn, imploring, tune I never had heard:
Boon of a bane—sweetly paining music.
'Tisn't every day a meter will make,
Holding my heart, such a fair impression.
Rhymeless, Háfiz' lines—and yet they impel,
Ardent in art, manly resolution—
Honeyed on the tongue, and sweetening grief,
Here are the hymns not to be resisted.
Omar barren reason banished and wed
Soon, in her stead, daunting vineyard's daughter.
Háfiz looked for pleasure—yet will he drink
Daily to find needed consolation.
What he loves eludes him: well do we know—
Many the ways—luring, then evading.

26. HÁFIZ-HAMMER I.79–82 TA 24: SCHUKUSTE SCHÜD GÜLI HAMRA WE GESEHT BÜLBÜL MEST

x/ x/ x/ x/
x/ x/ x/x
x/ x/ x/ x/
x/ x/x

Behold the rose in crimson bloom,
The nightingale is drunken:
You wise, who love the great Today,
Drink well, and freely!

The building of Remorse that we
Had made appeared a fortress—
Yet now—a crystal goblet—how
Completely shivered!

So bring the wine! Before the throne
Of Him that hears our wishes,
The sober, drunkard are alike,
And prince and watchman.

Because I have to leave behind
This little inn, two-gated,
My course of life may just as well
Be low as lofty.

We cannot live without our share
Of worry and of sorrow:
For us, upon the Day of Fate,
Was woe determined.

The Nought and Being never ought
Disturb the lightsome-hearted—
The end of every splendor is
Annihilation.

The Asaph-wealth and East-wind horse,
The lore of bird-world language
When lost, were sought to no avail;
The king had nothing.

Maintain the straighter way of earth,
And don't wing farther upward.
The arrow flying high will fall,
By dust be covered.

And how will tongue of writer-pen,
O Háfiz, ever thank you?
From mouth to mouth your wingéd words
Like wind are flying.

Reply

Good Asaph, grand vizier, had wealth
And loved it to distraction.
Yet wind-command and learnéd chirp
Proved no more able

To last; for Solomon—and one
Who knew that he knew nothing
(A Greek, the deepest mind of all)—
Were men, and mortal.

And so the Venerable Bede,
A noted Christian writer,
Portrayed the lives of us that die
In vivid likeness:

A bird imagine, he had asked,
Who'd flown into a palace;
He entered through one doorway black,
Flew out another.

He's free of bitter winter blast
And sheltered for a moment.
Yet oh, how brief the indoor stay
Before the leaving!

A theologian Bede had been,
A famed ecclesiastic.
But Háfiz' two-doored inn conveyed
A kindred wisdom.

By blue-cowled pious he had been
Reviled for love of pleasure.
Yet when he spoke of death and life
The soul took notice.

27. HÁFIZ-HAMMER I.84–85 TA 26: SULFESCH HESAR DIL BEJEK TAR MUJEST

/x /x /x /x

How a single hair will draw a
Thousand hearts to love your tresses!
From the musk the myriad winds will
Bring we've no escape remaining.
So that for the hope of fragrance
Every soul to you be offered,
Locks of hair are freely loosened,
Yet afar from all admirers.
And because my moon-belovéd
Bears the brows that, like the crescent
Viewed, will soon by cloud be hidden,
I'm the fool of melancholy.
Wine of many lovely colors
Had the tavern-boy decanted—
See the rare and rainbow painting
Of the many splendors melded.
When you pour it, pleasant gurgling
Sounds from out the long-necked bottle:
What a rare and spheric music
Had the singer tuned! the pious
In the transport of their dancing
Have their Ha! and Hu! forgotten.
Wise the ones who, lower conduct
Of the world bereft beholding,
Quickly have withdrawn, instructed,
Uttering no word about it.
Those who hate the bitterness of
Love, and head for pleasure only,
Try to don the pilgrim garb while
Shunning the required ablutions.

Reply

Learn the saying of the Sufis:
"Ha!" betokening "the Living,"
"Hu!" or He, the God, or Allah.

Dancers in ecstatic passion
Cry "He lives!" that all may hearken
And, with body, soul awakened,
Feel the wonder-heart that moved them
Strengthened by the Great Surrender.
As with Háfiz, wine-imbiber,
So the cool blue flute of Rumi,
Welling up the spring that felt a
Mortal dormancy to rarest
Radiance of wide awareness,
Will the soul reshape in beauty
Through the blood in love arising
As a bridegroom that awakens
Or a runner that, empowered
With a sunlike bliss in travel,
Racing westward, feels he quickly
Will the whirling wind outdistance.
Aye! Ha, hu! He lives, and living,
Gives the blessing of a brother
Singing in beloved oneness
What the stars afar engender
When, in flames that seem to sunder
Peace with bursting heart-explosion,
These convey to farthest reaches
Of a bounty-space unbounded
Elements that new-combining
Rouse the mind, the heart that, beating,
Moves the feet of me, a Sufi,
Who would dance, with vivid versing,
Lasting praise of breath to utter,
Clapping hands to echo thunder
Storms awaking in the Heaven
Setting free the rain of Mercy.

28. HÁFIZ/HAMMER I.87 TA 28: DER IN SEMANE REFIKI KI CHALI ES CHILET EST

/x x/ x/ x/ x/ x/x
/x /x x/ – /x /x /x

Should you today require a trusty friend, companion,
Raise a goblet of wine—board the ship of singing.
Go by yourself; you'll find a single means of rescue—
Take the glass—in your life, *that*'s the highest value.
I'm an inactive man, yet don't lament the problem:
Many sages possess wisdom, lacking action.
Prudently look at this, our lámentable passage:
All the boast of the world—wholly vain and idle.
Cheeks in delight to kiss!—and that was all I'd hoped for—
Death however will slit life's too-fragile purse string.
Hair of the moon embrace, abandon star-divining—
Lunar fortune forget, Saturn's gloomy portent. . . .
Sober, our Háfiz? No, like *that* you'll never find him.
He will always be drunk—so had Fate ordained it.

Reply

Wavery, winding line—a wayward frame I'd name it:
Rhythm wobbles a lot—toper, hobbling homeward.
What do we make of this: a cautionary portrait?
Is it pitiable? Vagrant, slipping, sliding?
Many prefer, I know, an allegoric vision:
Wine is ardor for God, drunken mind an emblem
Showing a finer heart in swelling aspiration.
Think of drunken Mejnún, often called a madman:
Strange, to a maiden lending all his vital power—
Yet to some he appeared holy in devotion.
Faint is the borderline between profane and sacred:
Body, soul are entwined, rapt affection blended.
What did the poet mean? I'm bad at star-divining.
Let the quarrel go on. Misty moon is hidden.

29. HÁFIZ-HAMMER I.88–90 TA 29: MARA ES CHIALĬ TU TSCHI PERVAĬ SCHERABEST

/x /x /x /x

While your image sways before me,
Why not try a little drinking?
"Be restrained," the tankard answers,
"Or the tavern will be ruined."

If within the lively vine-juice
Paradise may be discovered,
Yet, away! for tasty sherbet
Is but pain, without the Maiden.

Woe! she's fled and gone, the dear one—
And my eyes in tear-fall swimming,
With the beauteous form that wavers
Painted on the flowing water.

Keep alert, bright eye, awaken!
At his post whoever slumbers
By the flood-stream is imperiled
Every moment of his napping.

The Beloved had attempted
Here to walk unveiled and freely,
But when she espied a rival
She replaced the veil, well-fastened.

Ever since the rose the beauty
Of your cheeks, the gently dampened,
Saw, she felt oppressed with envy—
Rose-and-water distillation.

In the corners of my brain-life
Seek no wise advice or teaching;
Nothing will you find but strumming
Of the lute and zither-plucking.

What a long and hopeless highway
Is the road where love would lead us!
It would make the Sea of Heaven
Seem a mad mirage in wasteland.

Valleys fertile, hills are greening,
Come and sit beside the water
Not in vain and empty-handed,
For our time is flowing onward.

In my heart your face enkindled
Lights of love, above a hundred,
But (a stranger thing to think of)
These a hundred veils have covered.

O you fiery seed of heart-flame,
I, unfed by face-light gleaming,
See my heart, a heated dancer,
Long ago to dust-heap crumbled.

Yet may Háfiz still be drunken,
Roving-eyed and freely dreaming,
For with many bits of mischief
Is our time of youth enlivened.

Reply

When I felt the mood-swing alter
In the rambling of the speaker
And my thought began to wander,
Came a question: would a Persian

Who, attempting divination
Through a random line selected
From the venerated poet
And alighting on a passage

Where the pains of love are plainest,
When affected by depression
Face the music and apply it
To his unrelenting problem?

Often no solution's given,
Not a gleam of hope enkindled,
Naught but louring cloud-embankments
And a frowning woe predestined.

Should one read a little farther?
Or would this be counted cheating?
Is the wizard horoscopic
Inconsistent, downright doubtful?

Well, the Bible, the *Aeneid,*
And the vast Qur'an resplendent
Veer analogously into
Unpredictable dilemmas.

For the meaning of a saying
Will require a kind of seeing,
And imagination ever
Will be requisite for wisdom.

30. HÁFIZ-HAMMER I.90–92 TA 30: KENUN KI BER KEFĬ GUL DSCHAMĬ BADEĬ SAFEST

/x x/x x/
x/ x/x
/x /x x/
x/ x/x

See how the wine bubbles up
In rosy goblet,
Oh, the nightingale song
We hear from bushes!

Gather your lyrics in hand
And wander fieldward,
Now's a terrible time
For schoolboy homework.

Flee from the men of the world
To hermit Anka:
Kaf to Kaf, we will hear
That name, rejoicing.

Drunken, the provost proclaimed
The latest fatwa:
Wine-consuming? Far worse
Were handout-asking.

Lighter or cloudier wine
Will all be welcome;
What's the cupbearer-gift
But grace abounding?

Who is comparing my verse
To others' writing?
That is likening gold
To woven rushmats.

Quiet, O Háfiz, and keep
Secure the word-wealth:
Watchful be, and alert
To loaners' cheating.

Reply

Anka, Simúrg, would I sing!
Upon the mountain
Kaf, surrounding the world,
He lives, unending.

Circumferential the rock,
The hermit-dwelling.
Yet a center is he,
The highest bird-life:

Bravely inviolate mind
To vision faithful,
Kept from pressure of crowds,
Their sweaty rancor.

Mentor of Háfiz and me,
To Spirit open,
Strong in sunshine and cloud,
With eye of lightning.

He is the "earthly Buraq,"
Unviewed, secluded,
Sphere-concentered in thought
And filled with heaven.

Opened, the eyes of the bird:
In burst refulgent,
Glory known at the height—
An angel stirring.

Gabriel only, I feel,
Smaragdine-feathered,
Perched on Lote-tree will know
Simurgal wisdom.

31. HÁFIZ-HAMMER I.95–96 TA 33: EGERTSCHI ARSĬ HUNER PISCHĬ JAR BI EDEBEST

x/ x/ x/ x/ x/
/xx /xx /x
x/ x/ x/ x/ x/
/xx /xx /

Your merits to parade before your friends
Ever so brazenly—stop it:
O tongue, be silent!—ev'n if you command
Purest Arabian prose.

Perí her face of heaven turns away;
Only the Div, who's a demon,
Amazed and flaming-eyed has branded me.
Ah, what a wonder it is!

You cannot ask why heaven chose to lend
Favor to spirits unworthy.
A lack appears the prime criterion
Here for the lending of grace. . . .

Indeed! but no one in this meadow knew
Ever the rose to be thornless—
In even Prophet-lamp flew up the sparks,
Evil, of Abu Laháb.

I wouldn't buy for half a barleycorn
Cloister or home for the needy.
The tavern bench is *my* cathedral dome,
And, for my dwelling, the glass.

In my delighted eye you're shining bright,
Vine's lovely daughter! Your features
In charming goblet-garment comely veiled,
Clothed in the grape-skin before.

When you in sorrow seek a means to heal,
Hunt where the heart will take pleasure:
You'll find it in a flask well-filled with wine—
Aye, or a chinaware cup.

Was I unwise, good Master, so to boast?
Didn't I merit your favor?
And now, when I am—granted—rather drunk,
Ev'n to be brash isn't bad.

The wine! bring more! For this will Háfiz yet
Daily continue requesting—
While he at dawn can wail in long lament—
Later, at midnight, will pray.

Reply

Let those who will, be merely wise:
Mystery comes in shutting eyes.
Tones countless from unbounded skies
The coldened wizard hears arise.

Delight in silent pride belies
A restive quester's idle whys.
More violent than highest cries
A triumph, riant, spied in sighs.

Perí, Muse, Houri, you endue
The spire of iris! Loud abound
The lightnings whitening the ground:

O gladdened glance in bolder blue
By drumming thunder nourished through
Trees-Arteries!—my Sky-Heart—pound!

32. HÁFIZ-HAMMER I.100–101 TA 36: EGERTSCHI BADE FORHBANSCH WE BAD GÜLRIS ÉST

x/ x/ x/x x/
x/ x/ x/x x/
x/ x/ x/x x/
x/x x/x

Although the wine may gladden the heart,
Although the wind with blossom bestrew,
Yet drink not, you! to strum of the lute—
For keen is the watcher.

And if, mayhap, a friend or a flask
Should come to hand, be prudent, I pray!
Be sparing, careful, pouring a drink—
The times are alarming.

Within the roomy sleeve of your cowl,
Alert, concerned, your glass you may hide,
The times are dark and crimsoning, like
The eye of the bottle.

The marks of wine that spatter my cowl
I'd wash away with tears if I could.
The age of moderation has come—
A season for fasting.

The run of life is blood-dripping steel—
Behold, like raindrops falling to earth,
The gleaming head of high Nushirwán,
Crown royal of Párviz.

Renouncing all the goods of the world,
In this our era, seek no repose.
The purest wine such vessel will hold
Is dreg-heavy, clouded.

O Háfiz, you have conquered with song
The mode of Persia, then of Iraq;
Tebrís and Bághdad—they will be next,
And others will follow.

Reply

(1)

A new regime Mubáriz ud-Dín
Inaugurated: woe to the ones
Who love the inn! Their banquet will now
        Be shortened or canceled.

We raise our hands for Abu Ishâq,
The sadly ousted comrade of those
Anacreontic topers of whom
        Our bard was enamored.

Yet why lament? The lute on the page
Is tuned, and proved. The troubadour-luck
Will not run out. The conqueror comes!—
        The crowd will confirm it.

(2)
"FORTUNE PLANGO VULNERA" FROM *Carmina Burana* (TR. MB)

My plaint is of the pain that flows,
Crying, from the eyes.
Rebellious Luck retracted those
Presents I would prize.
For true it is, a forelock she
Has, that you may find.
But if you miss it you will see
Baldness all behind.

On Fortune's royal throne I'd sat,
Favored and elate,
Enwreathed and crowned with blossoms that
Friends are lent by Fate.
Once flourishing and raised on high,
Happy were my days.
Now fallen from the summit, I
Wail my former ways.

The wheel of fortune turns, and I
Sink, diminished, less,
As if ejected from the sky.
See, His Mightiness,
The King, that on the peak of pow'r
Dwells—let him beware:
Queen Hécuba, the Ilian flow'r—
Killed! and who will care?

(3)
COMMENT ON "Fortune Plango Vulnera"

Moody, abstracted, Lady Luck
Absentmindedly
Revolves the wheel: the gleams to muck
Turn—so, too, will we.

Bibamus, moriendum est.
Die? Let's have a drink.
Love while you live—that guide's the best.
Rise before we sink.

Shave Plato's beard with Ockham's blade.
Here is the cheer for which we're made.

33. HÁFIZ-HAMMER I.103–104 TA 38: AIBĪ RINDAN MEKÜN EI SAHIDĪ PAKISE SÜRÜSCHT

x/ x/ x/ x/ x/x
x/ x/ x/ x/ x/

You pious one, do *not* defame the drinker—
His sins aren't credited to your account.
If I am good—or bad—just you be quiet:
A man will reap whatever he had sown.
I'll not abandon hope that God be gracious,
You cannot know who's damned and who is blest!
A loving friend will know the drunk, the sober—
A church and mosque are each the house of love.
And not alone from purity I've fallen,
My father paradise already lost.
My head I to the taverner surrendered—
"So bow your head!" I say to envy dull.
The Garden's lovely, true, but you must relish
The meadow shadow and the greening grove.
What long ago was in the book indited
You know. Do not rely on pious deeds.
Glass touching lips, upon your death-day, Háfiz,
With bliss on lip, you'll rise to heaven high.
If so you are inclined, fine inclination!
If this remain your custom, custom wise!

Meum est propositum in taberna mori
ubi vina proxima morientis ori.
Tunc cantabunt laetius angelorum chori:
Deus sit propitius isti potatori.
—medieval lyric cited by Hammer in a note

I propose at death to be in the tavern laid,
Near the dying mouth for me let the wine be made.
May the choirs of angels sing: bliss will never fade.
Merciful be God the King; drinkers He will aid.
—Latin lyric in Hammer's note

Reply

The helpful Háfiz, Hammer, here had offered
Two medieval hymns, of East and West,
To ample Bacchic imbibition-wisdom,
That whoso wills to drink may solace have.
For church and mosque are charitable—insight
That many pious worshipers forget
Who, eager to correct the flaws of others,
The way to favor darken for the weak.
And who are strong? Let mosque and church be humble,
Nor steal the judge-prerogatives of Him
Whose verdict, by the mercy-angel tempered,
No mortal, fallible, can prophesy.

34. HÁFIZ-HAMMER I.104–105 TA 39: KENUM KI MIDEMID ES BOSTAN NESIMĬ BEHISCHT

/x x/x x/
x/ x/x
/x x/x x/
x/ x/x

Here is the paradise-breath
From garden wafting.
Nothing will keep me from wine—
The heaven-maiden.

Why shouldn't beggarmen be
Both proud and lordly?
Isn't the heaven their tent?
The field their ballroom?

Listen: the meadow declaims
Her Maytime lyric.
People with money in mind
Are not the wisest.

Freshen your heart with the wine!
The world is filled with
Buildings they make when our bones
Convert to mortar.

Never expect of your friend
That he be faithful.
Neither is holy the flame
In church lamps burning.

Pointless to blacken my name
For drink-indulgence.
Who on his forehead can know
What fate has written?

Turn not your footstep away
From Háfiz' gravesite.
If he be sunken in sin,
He'll trust in heaven.

Reply

Ritual burial they
Who'd scorned the drinker,
Much as he'd feared, would deny!
The final strophe

Came to the aid of the bard,
Persuading mockers.
People who cited the lines
Were vindicated.

Wine is in Eden allowed—
Of higher savor,
Freed of contingent effect:
The holy essence.

Many the plagues he would reap
In lover-sorrow—
Even in drinking he'd feel
Beleaguered, battered.

Poetry physicked the mind,
A friend in trial.
Yet in the mosque and at court
Were woes awaiting.

Slighting the lamps? Ill-advised—
Ill-tempered, hasty.
Often the mosque and the church
He praised together.

Getting defensive is on-
ly nervous reflex.
Yet am I cheered when I read
The *Sta viátor:*

Turn not your footstep away
From Háfiz' gravesite.
If he be sunken in sin,
He'll trust in heaven.

35. HÁFIZ-HAMMER I.126–27 TA 53: SI KIRIH MERDUMI TSCHESCHM NICHESTE DER CHUN EST

/xx /xx /xx /xx /xx /x
/xx /xx / – /xx /xx /

Weeping and moaning inflaming my eyes with the carmine of bloodflow,
Take a good look! to such grief sight of a lover you've brought.
Blood becomes rutilant wine when it's poured from the glass of the griever—
Drink to the health of the lips, also the drinking man's eye.
After the sun in the east from your dwelling has early arisen,
Rays from my forehead stream out, as of the dawn's lucky star.
Taking my heart in your hand, you, my friend, like a cedar-tree graceful,
Say but a heartening word!—lovably flowing, that word.
Taverner, grant me a réspite, and bring a few goblets, returning—
For, by the turning of earth, I to the ground have been felled.
Since the unfortunate moment when out of my hands fled the maiden,
As in the Orus the wet hem of my garment is drenched.
How could it happen that ever my innermost essence be gentled?
I have no choice on my own, or to be happy or sad.
Dead to the life of the world in desire for the vanished beloved,
Háfiz a beggar is turned, yearning for wealth of Karún.
Hérhad his melody sang of the lips of kind Shírin, caressing;
Think of Mejnún, of that heart—captured in Laila's long hair.

Reply

Stories recurrent—no end to the tale while the world-ball is rolling:
Hero Mejnún do we view, tasting the plaguiest woe.
Prey of the innermost coil of the nine-headed serpent rapacious,
Never the victim escapes—nine are the walls of the jail.
There is a window, however, in each of the spheres of the prison:
Moments will come when the fire caught in the soul, meeting light,
Feels the old freedom preceding the time when the Adam-encasement
Weighted, with freighting of clay, nightingale-singers on earth.
Wine of the ardor of hero-affection, untamable fervor,
Came to the aid of our bard. So it assisted Mejnún:
Banished, enisled in a swither of sand-wrack, ungratified yearning,
Famished he sat on a dune, tracing the name of his love.
Stormy simoom would in blinding-hot blazing, forlorn with frustration,
Quickly the name of the lost maiden insanely erase.

Yet would the lover, who'd never surrender except to the Highest,
Write, as a poet inspired, daily and nightly her name
Ninety-nine times in a faith-laden testament lent to the ages:
Hail, undeflected Mejnún—sisyphal doom of desire!

36. HÁFIZ-HAMMER I.127–29 TA 54: MERDÜMĬ DIDEĬ MA DSCHÜS BERUCHET NASIR NIST

x/ x/ x/x x/ x/
x/ x/ x/ x/ x/x

The pupil of my eye will avoid your face—
My heart, astray, remembers you, however.
My tears require the holiest pilgrim garb
Though daily tainted by the heart-blood tingeing.
Do *not* reject the coin of a lover's heart—
He cannot pay you in the current mintage.
But one who is of confident mind and brave
Attains at length your lofty cypress stature.
The miracle-ability Jesus had
Could not compete with yours—your lips, the honeyed.
My love's aflame, if never a sigh be heard—
My branding, you will grant, I bear with patience.
The rarest Eden-bird in a cage is kept,
That he may not be striving, you to rival.
When I at first caught sight of your tresses' charm
I cried, "Entrapment!—unrelenting tangle!"
Not Háfiz 'tis alone that will pine for you;
For can there be a man who lacks that longing?

Reply

A pilgrim secret lies in the deep ideal
Engendering-enlivening his art,
And knowing this I'll write of the fire I feel:
The marvel-rhythm is the hiker's heart.

With discipline, tradition, we nobly start:
Let melody unwind from spool to spiel,
In single ring the elements four anneal,
That all be one in sun, and none apart.

The apple, avid-Ámor, the charming dart:
The man will upright stand, who had to kneel.
Is love a sorrow? Pain is a double smart:
Our tears are dew, our vale we new-reveal.

The molten ore, once frore in the old ordeal,
Re-lava'd, heats what frigid fates congeal!

37. HÁFIZ-HAMMER I.130–31 TA 56: SAKIA AMEDENĬ IID MUBAREK BADET

x/ x/ x/ x/
x/ x/

We bless you, tavern host—the fest
Has now arrived!
Do not forget the promise made—
The time is nigh.
Go, cupboy, greet the Daughter of
The Vine, and say:
Belov'd, appear! desire and hope
Have banished grief!
I marvel how, sequestered, you
So long have kept
Both heart and hand from suitors, all
By sorrow tried.
Thank God! the autumn wind has not
Inflicted harm
Upon the cedar tree, or beech,
The jasmine, rose. . . .
The evil eye remain afar!
From torment fierce
Your native constellation had
Preserved you well—
The elders gladdened, now you're here:
Let any heart
That fails to wish you every joy
Be sore dismayed.
Don't, Háfiz, let that Noah's ark
Escape your hand,
Nor let the grounding of your bliss
Be washed away!

Reply

The month of Ramazan is done,
And Shuja comes
Who loved the Daughter of the Vine
And set her free!
That Muhtasíb could not quite kill

The garden life
Which, light to love, is new-upsprung
May God be praised!
The fasting time, dominion of
The Wine Police—
Quite finished, and our Eden-tree
Put forth her fruit.
Our Father Noah, who of old
Invented wine,
But little knew that he had found
An ark as well,
Which through an age of dire constraint
Might safely bear
The spirit dovelike to the land
Above the Flood.
The Daughter of the Vine has this
In common with
A flute of Rumi: both will make
The dancing feet
And sleeping soul awake to feel
The Garden-life.
The blood aroused, we cry within:
Hu! Ha!—He lives!

38. HÁFIZ-HAMMER I.133–34 TA 58: SUBUHDEM MURGHĬTSCHEMEN BA GÜLĬ NEVEHASTE GUFT

/xx /xx /xx /xx /xx /x
/xx /xx / – /xx /xx /

Said in the morning the bird of the meadow to Rose newly-budded:
  "Don't be so cold and reserved; plenty of roses like you!"
Smiling, the flower replied, "Though the truth you are certainly telling,
  Talk as ungentle as *that* hardly befits one in love.
Someone who never with cheek in the dust brushed the innkeeper's threshold
  Won't with the fragrance of love, even of friendship be blest.
Never expect you will get to the rubies in goblet embedded
  Till on your eyelashes tears hang like the pearls on a string."
Yesterday plainly I saw how the lovable East-wind a-wafting
  Swiftly disheveled the hair Hyacinth loved to display.
There in the Garden of Íram, I said, "Throne of Jémshid, pray tell me:
  Where's the world-mirroring cup?" "Ah, it is gone," he replied.
Language of love I no longer can hear from the tongue of the lovers—
  Taverner, bring us the wine! Chattiness bring to an end!
Reason and patience, for Háfiz, in hot-streaming tears are beflooded:
  There is no more he can do—lovers deep grieving must feel.

Reply

Nightingale, Rose are the stars of a long-running, many-act drama—
  Hyacinth often is hired, too, for a beautiful role.
East-wind's important: no matter how seemingly forceful, yet ever
  Ready aroma to bear, playful, a hair-lock to tease.
Íram had suffered, of old, catastrophic Qur'anic destruction;
  Therefore no miracle-glass—prophet, predictor—survives.
Emblem of elegy, yes—but the charm of the garden bucolic—
  Impudent flower and bird, witty and lyric at once—
Teardrops' pearl necklace and dust on the cheek as the price of the rubies
  Bedded in gold of the cup offered to comfort the weak—
All is a tapestry woven on gilded brocade ornamental,
  Humanized life overheard, fabled on Solomon's ring.
That is the remnant, Aladdin-like, felt of the fairy-tale magic
  Solomon knew when he rode Wind like the horse of a storm.
Let me not end before lauding once more the Ovidian distich,
  Brisker than wind of the spring, brushing the new-budded earth.

39. HÁFIZ-HAMMER I.136–38 TA 60: RUI TU KES NEDID WE HESARET RAKIB EST

x/ x/ x/ x/
x/ x/ x/ x/ x/x
x/ x/ x/ x/
x/ x/ x/x

No man has seen your countenance,
And yet a thousand rivals wait to meet you—
In early bud you're welcomed by
The nightingales, a thousand.

When I approach your dwelling place
Be not surprised, I beg, for where's the wonder?
Innumerable strangers live
Not far from here, as I do.

As far as I'm away from you—
I wish that no one had to keep that distance!
And yet the hope of pleasure feels
Quite near me, ever nearer.

The Muslim convent and the pub
Ought not to be misleadingly contrasted—
The face of the Beloved shines
Wherever one may find it.

Where pious men a holy work
Pursue with upright zeal and spirit eager,
Monastic bell will *there* resound
And *there* the cross be honored.

Is there a loved one who'd not think
The lover to be worthy of beholding?
I'm healthy—yet, if I were ill,
My Friend's nearby to aid me.

Our Háfiz' plaints anent his Friend
Were not, it seems, to empty wind-breath spoken—
For they're a well-known legend-book
And modern wonder-story.

Reply

The breadth of open-heartedness
May startle even Háfiz' daily reader.
The poet feels delight to see
Admirers of the Comrade.

The man is likened to a rose,
Recalling that in Sonnet One of Shakespeare—
As Will the beauty of the Friend
Had lauded from the outset,

Thus here the nightingales delight
In all the lauds to budding rose directed.
The ever-growing reign of love
Will soon include religion

As nightingale and rose provide
A body-spirit, God-and-human linkage.
The ardor in a lover's eye
A hermit learned by service—

The Christian and Islamic monk
United with the connoisseur of beauty
In zeal for what the Sun had made
That life to all is lending.

So Rumi and beloved Shams
(Who even had a name that aptly mirrored
The very *sun* that he appeared
In beauty to embody),

While joining in the dance of life
To praise the ardor of the flame-creation,
Will win applause in lyric joy
And hymn our Allah-Father.

40. HÁFIZ-HAMMER I.141–42 TA 64: CI GHAIB SI NASAR BECHUDA MISIPAREMET

/x /xx /x /x /x

You, how distant! but be to God commended!
I'm consumed by my love and heart-devotion.
Be assured that my hand will love your garment
Till my own is entombed in earth below me.
Lead me now to the altar of your eyebrows,
That my hands in a morning pray'r be lifted.
Need I even to Babel go, to Hárut,
Anything would I do, to bring you *with* me.
Lend me only the strength, so will my teardrops
Fall, the pearls of the eye, your feet bedewing.
See, my tears in a stream flow on, unhalted—
Now, may seeds of my love in you sprout upward!
Though my blood you have shed, the parting-sorrow
Oh so quickly removed, with such a dagger. . . .
Faithless doctor, you're glad to see me dying!
Go—the boy that awaits you is impatient.
Wine and handsome beloved hardly suit you,
Háfiz, yet—you are left to your destruction.

Reply

Great the measure of Háfiz' desperation!
Don't forget that the angels Hárut, Márut
(Masters, they, of a doubtful kind of magic)
Sought (though vainly) to tempt the perfect Zohra,
Who, now star of the morning, star of evening,
From the fourth of the spheres (the home of Jesus)
Pours pure light on the lost and lonely roamer
While the angels in Babel-well are fettered.
Here we've one of the more disturbing lyrics
Háfiz wrote, with a will to castigation
Aimed not only at one who, unresponsive,
Raised the walls of a dudgeon, mental dungeon,
But, additionally, a deep self-hatred.
He has likened the eyebrows of the comrade

Boldly to the *mihráb* or prayer-alcove
Where a worshiper's thought is well directed
Straight to Mecca, the sacred place of Allah.
Lend the sufferer, pray, a word of mercy.

41. HÁFIZ-HAMMER I.142–44 TA 60: JA RABB SEBEBÍ SASKI JAREM BESELAMET

/xx /xx /xx /xx /xx /x
/xx /xx / – /xx /xx /

Lord! may You grant that my comrade return in a state of well-being,
Free me as well from reports, rumors that I am distraught.
Bring me the dust that my Friend in his wide-ranging travel had gathered—
Dust that upon him had lain—ah! what a salve for the eyes!
Tresses and beauty-mark, beard-down and cheeks, and his face, and that stature!—
All six directions are blocked—stopping escape from my Friend.
Even today I am still in his power, have mercy upon me!
I will tomorrow be dust!—what of your mercy-tears *then*?
You, that with driest of words would the nature of loving interpret,
Go, God be with you! To such, I can have nothing to say.
Pitiable! don't lament any longer the Friend's cruel sword-thrust:
Some will extract further wealth even from victims who've died.
Now your blue cowl set aflame! for the curve of the brows of the cupboy
Wrecked the *mihráb* in the mosque, right where the imam would pray.
Never would *I*, God forbid, for your harshness toward me accuse you:
Wrongs from the loved one received ought to be counted benign.
Háfiz will end, here as ever, his tale with a mention of tresses:
These are the theme of his verse, till the Last Judgment arrive.

Reply

Here we've a troubadour portrait, a kind that is rarely considered:
Perfect, the gems of the frame—worshiped, the face of the Friend.
Dante, the bard Beatrician, had punished Brunetto Latini,
Making him run on the sand, barefoot in desert like hell,
Calling him one who in running appeared as a winner, not loser—
Irony horrid to hear, compliment right to despise—
What would he think of the Persian *trouvère* who exceeded Brunetto,
Pained by an ecstasy-wound, painting companionly love?
Why in our schools are the masterly martyrs like Háfiz unmentioned?
Homer and Vergil we know—ev'n Alexander the Great—
Monarch who'd sleep every night with the *Iliad* under his pillow—
Each lauded comrades in love; all were to Háfiz akin.
Tales of Euryalus, Nisus, to schoolboys in classroom were given:
Corydon—what can I say? Why then should Háfiz be shunned?

Lines Michelangelo wrote to a man—and they well might have perished—
Sappho's are mainly destroyed. Plato had named her "Tenth Muse"!
Who is the muse in the brave Sonnet Seventy-Eight of our Shakespeare?
He is the comrade of Will. Háfiz—*befriended*—awake!

42. HÁFIZ-HAMMER I. 144–45 TA 66: AN JARĬ DILNUVASEM SCHUKRIST BE SCHILKAJET

/xx /xx /xx /xx /xx /x
/xx /xx / – /xx /xx /

I must lament and yet thank, both at once, my most flattering comrades,
Hear then my tale if you feel wisdom in love may be yours.
I, unrewarded, unthanked, have, for one, many services rendered:
Never should person well served grant no acknowledgment, Lord!
We, with dry lips, the free-spirited—no one will offer us water—
All who might wisdom detect fled, long ago, from the land!
I, in the darkness of night, have lost track of the path I should travel—
You, from your corner—come forth!—bright constellation, to guide!
Nothing but horror and fear has encumbered each footstep I've taken:
Think of the wasteland ahead—mind the Unending, the Way.
No one can ever imagine an end to the path I must wander:
Right at the start you will find myriad stages to pass.
I from your door am not moving, no matter how many the insults:
Better than praise from a foe—chiding, for me, of a Friend.
Help will you get in your love when, like Háfiz, by heart you recite them—
All of the twice seven ways Holy Qur'an should be read.

Reply

Here a most grave revelation with firmness appears a conversion:
Hopeless the love for the Friend—therefore a road you must take
Leading to height that a spirit when questing can barely imagine,
Way that will comet-like wend, spiraling up to the stars.
Háfiz, he knew, had the meaning of one who had treasured the scripture—
Here declaration is made: "Yes, I recite it, and more."
Never before had I felt such mood of despair *de profundīs*—
Out of the depth came a cry: now must my journey begin!
Nothing I'd heard in the earlier lyrics could ever prepare me—
Even with metaphor-height, mortal the loves and the wine.
All of a sudden the claim has been made that the words of the Prophet,
Read on the night when the strong Gabriel-Angel had won,
After a struggle protracted, the soul of Muhammad to Allah,
Conquered our Háfiz at last, pilgrimage long to begin.
Now more than ever I feel how the dawn-light of spirit-portrayal
Meant that the poet would be centuries treasured and loved.

43. HÁFIZ-HAMMER I.146–47 TA 67: MUDAMEM MEST MIDARED NESIMĬ DSCHAADĬ KISUJET

/x /xx /x
x/ x/ x/ x/x

I will ever be drunken
When breathing curly locks' aroma—
I will ever be flustered
When taking in your wizard glances.
After such a protracted
And patient waiting, when, Lord, may I
Near the altar of eyebrows
Enkindle, burn, my vision-candle!
I have held it in honor—
The pupil of the eye, in blackness,
For it holds the impression,
In spirit, of your mark of beauty.
Should you wish, of a sudden,
That we behold the life eternal,
Simply say to the East-wind
That it may lightly raise your cheek-veil.
Should you wish, of a sudden,
That we behold the world discarnate,
Loose your tresses—a myriad
Of spirits hangs on every hair-end.
I and East-wind together
Are miserable fools, demented—
I bewitched by your eye-light
And he by aromatic tresses.
Lofty spirit of Háfiz!—
Of both our worlds—the lower, higher—
Nothing must he adore but
The humble dust upon your threshold.

Reply

(1)

Veiled is Heaven, yet open
To vision when the wind has lifted

Ev'n for only a moment
The mystic veil of the Beloved.
Dust employed for a salve in
The treatment of the eye is common
When the dust-grains are taken
From sainted mage's holy gravestone.
Here the noble Adored is
In body and in spirit sacred:
Dust new-come from the dwelling
Attained a healing marvel-power.
Háfiz' link to the East-wind—
Arising from their adoration,
That of poet for eye-charm
And that of wind for bold aroma—
Joins the body and spirit
In breeze and in the celebrator.
Souls that hang on the hair-locks
Come down from higher life in homage:
One who, like the Beloved,
Controls them with a conjuration
Blends the worlds in a mercy
Like Allah's vernal rain, or like the
Sending down of the Prophet
To raise from dust what long lay barren:
Green, the hue of Muhammad,
Portending life renewed for lovers.

(2)

Trochee, dactyl, and trochee,
And then a fourfold iamb-answer.
That's the classical practice,
Perfected further by the Persian:
Mix the feet in the scansion,
So rhythms differ every time you
Pen, impulsive, a poem
With lift—and lulling, rolling motion.
Twenty-eight, I have noticed,
May well be named a favored number:
Well, whatever the motive,
I daily revel in the rhythm.

44. HÁFIZ-HAMMER I.147–48 TA 68: EL MINNET LILLAHĬ KI DER MEIKEDEH BAS EST

/xx /xx /x
x/x x/x
x/ x/ x/ x/ x/x

Praise the Almighty! The tavern
Is open, and welcome,
For by that door I may evade my sorrows.

Everything whirls in confusion,
Chaotic in ardor,
And yet this wine is real, not allegoric.

Wine-cups are drunken and stubborn
And mockingly minded,
And I, in contrast, limp and weak, imploring.

Torments of tresses I cannot
Relate to you briefly:
The tale of them will make a longer story.

Hair-locks of Laila would burden
The spirit of Méjnun—
The soles of Áyaz, Máhmud's face would trouble.

Shut is my eye, never opened—
For I am a falcon
Since blinding light from you has lit the morning.

Whoso approaches your kaaba,
The place of the holy,
Must pray before your brows that are the qibla.

Friends, if you ask about Háfiz,
The poor one, examine
The candle ever melting while it's burning.

Reply

Wine of the singer-salvation
Is not allegoric,
For so the poet told, and no mistaking.

Two, though, will never be parted:
Our love—and religion.
So Méjnun-Romeo is yet a martyr.

Nothing will quiet the pious
Who, sunlike in Allah,
Know love as warming light and life transforming.

Waiting and burning and living
And singing and dying,
We laugh and weep—in cheerful splendor perish.

Hegel had taught me in Háfiz
To laud the parrhesia:
I am a sun, a psalmer, and a center.

Hating the shame of the petty—
Dissolving and falling,
The blood drums thunder in a rainy passion.

What is a madness, be-jinning?
The reason defeated.
O help me in my weak and lonely moment!

Tempting a blink among billions
Of galaxy atoms,
Are self and envy not a devil-dwelling?

Candid a laughing, a candle,
A hot lamentation,
The wasting—and the white, the smile, the silence.

45. HÁFIZ-HAMMER I.171–73 TA 83: KES NIST KI UFTADE AN SULFÍ DU TANIST

/xx /xx /xx /xx /xx /x
/xx /xx / – /xx /xx /

None to the double-tress, lovely, can ever resist being victim—
    Where can I go to avoid nets of misfortune and traps?
Often I think that your face may be called of the God-face a mirror—
    Yes! I'm declaring the truth, not a distortion at all.
One from the convent has warned me your face cannot merit such ardor:
    Isn't he shamed before God?!—Even more shamed before *you*!
Bitter the fate that we share, O bemoan it, you candle of musk-wind—
    Hidden the heat of the glow, filling us both, to consume!
God be my witness—and God is far more than sufficient for witness—
    Precious the tears that are shed, blood of the martyrs are they.
See, the narcissus inclined to your eye, for it craved a caressing—
    Weaker, the eye of the flow'r lacking your love-life and shine!
Let me now swear before God—you must *not* loose the hood, curl the tresses—
    Else will we struggle all night, envious East-wind and I.
Yesterday, quickly, he left. Then said I, "Unreliable, fickle!"
    "Ah, you're mistaken," claimed he, "faithfulness' time is long gone."
Now that your eye's robbed the heart of the monks, of the very most pious,
    Isn't my following *you* really disgraceful to me?
Kindly come back! With your heart-lighting countenance vanishing sadly,
    Joy from my circle of friends ever is banished as well.
After the innkeeper entered our circle, your latter disciple,
    Onto our heads from the Lord holier myst'ry came down.
Men who are wise comprehend that the ones who are timid should never
    Look at the sun and cry out, I am the fountain of light!
Look! taking care of the stranger was always accounted a duty.
    Say, is that law of the soul foreign, perhaps, in your town?
Arrows of shame and reproach will descend upon one so beloved—
    Nor will the arrow of fate shield of a hero deflect!
Now in the room of the monk and as well in the cell of the Sufi
    Never *mihráb* will be found, save for the arc of your brows.
Should you be dipping your hand in the swift-running heart-blood of Háfiz,
    Flee from the wrath of the Lord, lest he avenge the Qur'an!

Reply

(1)

Here we've the star of a play of soliloquies, daily in making—
    That's why the final two lines, often deleted from texts,
Odd though they be in defense of a deity made to seem petty,
    Ought to be printed, as here—fuller, the portrait of one
Who, in the dizzying hues of the scroll of a feeling unfolded,
    Diary lines will compose, noting a life while it's led.
Even the image-hyperbole (all of the monks who are tempted;
    Envy of East-wind—*mihráb*—alcove for eyebrows adored)
Heightens the rush and the urge of competitive impulses warring:
    Gentle, self-pitying love, tense if neglected, ignored—
Quickly revived like a sudden up-gusting of winds that were dormant,
    Then, disappointed again, turning to metaphor-threat!
Shakespeare, in *Sonnets*, would prove, but a couple of centuries later,
    Háfiz a precedent set—writing of self might combine
Quester-confession with features of novel and lyric and drama:
    Much is chaotic, and yet—hear from a man who has *loved*!

(2)

One of the earliest lyrics I rendered will show an intruder,
    Thief of the heart of each monk, fickle as ever was known.
Peril he poses, undoing the hood of his cowl of a Sufi:
    East-wind and Háfiz will fight, roselike aroma to win.

Ah, so familiar! But—oh! I was startled that Joseph von Hammer
    Wouldn't face up to the fact: rose-boy he'd turned to a girl—
Coldly inconstant and faithless, the stereotypic allurer
    Liked by the bards of the West. Háfiz again is betrayed.

Poet of Persia, your lovers, laboriously re-engendered,
    Maidened by Hammer, arise! Eden will know them anew:
Quick operation, and painless!—enlightening reader and critic:
    Praise to the mercy of Truth! Blessing, and say ye, Ah-*men*!

46. HÁFIZ-HAMMER I.176–78 TA 85: NASARĬ PIRĬ MUGHAN MUDSCHIBĬ ISCH U TURBEST

/xx /xx /
x/ x/x

Cupbearer's image can lend
        Us joy and comfort—
Precious the water and air
        In tavern-garden.
See how the honored will pay
        His thought their homage.
More to explain in my lines
        Might seem quite shameless.
Tales that of Eden may tell,
        And spheres of heaven,
Shimmering light will diffuse
        By wine engendered.
Mine be the spice-needing mind
        Desiring wine-gems.
Misers I leave to prefer
        Their gold and silver.
Right on our foreheads the quill
        Our lot has written
Leading to heaven or hell,
        To pub or kaaba.
Serpents protecting the wealth—
        Oh, end the fables!
Never could even Laháb
        Defeat the Prophet!
Pearl of the purest—the man
        Of spirit-greatness,
Virtue that can't be acquired
        But lent by nature.
Favored with guidance of God
        Upon this roadway,
Háfiz' good mood is improved
        In dark and daylight.

Reply

Men of great spirit are praised,
For these have courage,
Trusting that they will attain
Their fated mission.
Prophet Muhammad had faced
A trying rival,
Patriarch Abu Lahāb,
A grumpy cousin.
Abu Lahāb had a wife
Who added mischief,
Strewing her thorns in the wild,
Unwelcome desert
There, where the Prophet, she knew,
Would walk, and barefoot.
These reprehensible foes
Are named, are labeled—
Never a culprit so cursed
In Holy Kóran.
Chapter: the fourth from the end—
And Joseph Hammer,
Rhyming the lines in a song
Will versify it:

"Weak are the hands of Laháb, and his pride will alter.
His riches never did him any good,
He faces hell-fire, be it understood,
His wife will carry down a load of wood,
And her neck be oppressed by a fine palm-fiber halter."
—Sura 111 (translated by J. v. Hammer)

47. HÁFIZ-HAMMER I.180 TA 87: RUSE JEKSU SCHUD U ID AMED U DILHAS BERCHAST

x/ x/ x/ x/ x/ x/x

The fast is over! now the fest! our hearts uplifted,
The wine fermenting in the barrel: best prepare it!
It isn't time to hear the boring virtue-braggarts—
The time of joy and high desire's arrived for *drinkers*.
Does one who, like myself, drinks gladly merit chiding?
Is it a shame, a flaw in character, a blemish?
A drinker who is not a hypocrite, or liar,
Is better than a knave in convent cell monastic.
We want to do what's right, to no one bringing evil—
And what's forbidden we will never call permitted.
The wine is but the blood of vines, it isn't *your* blood—
So why erupt if we knock back some heady goblets?
It merits no reproval—no one has been injured:
If it's reprovable, go find the sin-free critic!
Forget the when and where, good Háfiz, if you're drinking—
Who cares for when and how, eternal things considered?

Reply

The line contrasting blood of vines to that of humans
Will loud resound within the hearing singer's thinking:
The tragedies brought on by wine-desire misguided
Are dwarfed in human life by sanguinary conflict.
In ranking sins we ought to ask: how many victims?
How large the carnage? Whether death has overtaken
The furthering of life, the goal of human morals—
Behold the query not ignorable, but foremost.
Von Hammer made in art, in splendid peroration,
A bold rhapsodic contrast: Háfiz he defended
For having sung the praise of love and wine together
In troubled times when Tamerlane with bloody conquest
(Incarnadine the wild portrayal made by Marlowe!)
To pride had offered up the sovereignty of nations.
Shed vineyard blood—and not the blood of breathing people.

48. HÁFIZ-HAMMER I.182–83 TA 89: HADISSĬ SERV KI GOJED BE PISCHĬ KAMETI DOST

/xx /xx /xx /xx /xx /x
/xx /xx / – /xx /xx /

Who'll be so bold as to mention the cedar in talk with a comrade?
Surely the cedar has stol'n form and comportment from *him.*
I would be even reluctant to think of the height of a cypress—
True, it grows freely and high, yet is self-centered as well.
Tale of the beauty-mark, tresses, the East-wind relates to the musk-plant—
That will explain why it strewed fragrant aromas abroad.
Curving, the line to be viewed on the lunar-bright face of the Comrade:
Is it the eyebrow—or wait—maybe the crescent new moon?
Oh, that the lover had myriad souls, who, so carefree, his head has
Thrown, like a polo-ball whirled, nearer a tress of the Friend.
Would you the wish of your heart by your lunar-bright Comrade see granted,
Do not, like Háfiz, run fast after the quick-tumbling head!

"Be like palms, benign, or be
Like the cypress, high and free."
—Saadi, quoted by Hammer in a footnote to poem 48

Reply

Double the problem confronted in hearing the lyric of Háfiz.
Trees that are lauded for height little of shade may provide.
Cypress, though slender and tall and in curvature graceful and charming,
Wide-spreading branches will lack; shadow for traveler—scant.
Hammer applauded the two-sided moralized equable portrait—
Saadi in speaking of trees offered analogous thought.
Goethe, however, in *Essays and Notes* to the *West-Eastern Dívan,*
Claimed that the "polo-ball head" often was downright absurd.
Odd that the poets in Persia so liked to apply it to people:
Well, were the choice up to me, cypresses I would prefer.

49. HÁFIZ-HAMMER I.183–85 TA 90:
SUCHAN SCHINASI NEI EI DILBERA CHATA INDSCHAST

x/ x/ x/ x/
x/ x/x
x/ x/ x/ x/
x/ x/ x/x

If you are puzzled by a word,
      You've made no error.
You heard it from a man of heart?
      Don't say it is an error.

This life won't make me bow my head—
      Nor yet the other!
The Lord be blest who in my head
      Such uproar has awakened.

Where hearts when ill may find repose
      I've no idea.
Though I am still, you hear, within,
      Unending cries of battle.

The shame-veil from my heart is flown—
      Where *are* you, singer?
Compose! Your melody will set
      At peace my heart-love martyred.

I've never been at all concerned
      With worldly dealings.
Your face alone the beauteous world
      Adorned for my beholding.

How often has your image kept
      My soul from sleeping—
A hundred nights I've drunk this wine
      Not found in any tavern.

My cell is badly spattered now,
      Besoiled by heart-blood:
It you would wash it out with wine,
      How deeply I'd be grateful!

The fiery heat my heart contains—
There's naught can quench it!
And that is why I'm so well loved
In Zoroaster-convent.

And did you hear, but yesternight,
The singer trilling?
My life-breath had escaped away,
But morning new-bestirred me.

For of your love my heart received
Transforming tidings:
My breast is now with longing filled,
With singing and with music.

The moment when to Háfiz came
The dear one's love-word,
His heart, a mountain in desire,
The message echoed loudly.

Reply

Frangor, non flector, Hammer claimed
Might be the motto
For Háfiz here, who will not bend
Until at length he's broken.

Said Hammer, here's "a bar of steel."
Yet I, in contrast,
Can feel the bar's half-molten yet,
The swagger notwithstanding.

Unswaying? Rather, subject to
A wildfire mood-swing.
The nights of liquor never brewed
Have skewed the balance.

The poet is more changing than
The Hammer portrait,
In every way far more alive
Than sublimated image.

The skiey blue of Sufi cowl
With wine bespotted,
Is worn by one whose heart on fire
Flamed Zoroaster-crimson.

The blue ideal and red of heat
Are pitched in battle—
He threw the veil of shame aside,
Displayed the inner fighting.

I hope the reader may forgive
A simple moral:
The spirit is a battlefield—
The war will not be over.

50. HÁFIZ-HAMMER I.190–93 DSCHIM 1: SESEDKI ES HAME DILBERAN SITANÌ BADSCH

x/ x/ x/ x/ x/ x/

'Tis fitting you from all the handsome tribute take,
For truly in the Land of Handsome you are king.
Your eyes have every heart of Turkestan bestirred,
From China, India, to hair-locks bearing gifts.
The whiteness of your face is brighter than the day,
The blackness of your hair is darker than the night.
How, then, shall this my malady be ever healed,
When to my heart from you no means of healing comes?
To Khizer's rill your slender mouth a sweetness lent—
The sugar cane of Egypt—near your lips, ashamed.
You're battering my soul, and why? you heart of stone!
Too tender far, my shattered heart, mere fragile glass.
How thin your narrow waist with little hair-length belt,
How flexible your body white as ivory!
Your beard-down Khizer, and your mouth the rill of life,
Your stature treelike, hair-thin waist, and wax-white breast.
For you, as for a treasure, yearns poor Háfiz' heart:
O were he but a slave, and to your threshold-dust!

———

To you, of beauty crown,
Appropriate is beauty's gift;
Your winelike-sparkling eyes
The heart of Turkestan uplift;
And ah! your curly hair
Draws China's, India's ware.

Day's radiance fades away
Before your face magnificent;
The darkness of your hair
Is with the midnight blackness blent;
What heart its health regains
If *you* don't heal the pains?

The rill of Khizer flows
As though from rosy lips it came;
The spices of your mouth
Shame Egypt with her sugar cane;
To me, so weak, brought low
And shattered, mercy show!

Your ever-slender waist,
Sublime your height and pure to see,
Your stature cypress-high,
Your limbs like bending ivory;
Your mouth will give new life
To one with illness rife.

Fresh down upon your chin,
So like the tender meadow-green;
Your jasmine-fragrant breast—
Of beauties all are you the queen!
If only Háfiz prove
Apt servant of your love!

—poem given in Hammer's commentary to Háfiz poem 50
(translated into German by Count Carl von Harrach)

Reply

(1)

In Persia, too, they love the kind of "blazon" hymn
That Edmund Spenser, Philip Sidney were to write
(A later style we find invented by Marot).
In Europe a tradition of ambivalence
Accrued to lyric listing of the body parts—
An entertaining topic. Many people think
Parodic humor came to dominate the work
That claimed, "My mistress' eyes are nothing like the sun"
(One hundred thirty, Shakespeare). Háfiz' blazoning
Would seem of all ironic shadow to be free;
But as in William's *Lieder*, where we cannot tell,

In any given lyric, if it be addressed
To William's cherished comrade or his lady dark
(These, in a drama fully worthy of the plays,
Contend for his affection, for he loves them both
Although they love each other—sweetly heating strife!),
So here the fond portrayal of the paragon
Shows either man or woman in the poet's mind.

(2)

More likely *man*, however, for there's been a trend
(Conformable to narrow sects-morality)
Of gender-alteration in the rendering
Of Háfiz' verse, and I would vote with Hammer here
And not with Carl von Harrach, though I like his lines—
Depicted is the *King* of Beauty, not the Queen.
And let me add that after reading Háfiz' work
Our expectation we may need to readjust
For beauty-goals portrayed in vaguely gendered traits:
A narrow waist, and fragrant hair, and ruby lips
Are found, in Háfiz' work, in women and in men.
And that is why a body blazoned in a verse
May readily be gender-switched and, even yet,
In this portrayal few if any changes made.
You'll maybe hear a Háfiz tune and quickly mark
No hint about the gender of the addressee.
Now here's a value statement, patently implied:
It's only love we (c)are about, and love is love.

51. HÁFIZ-HAMMER I.219–20 DAL 9: SALHA DIL TALEBĬ DSCHAMĬ DSCHEM ES MA KERD

x/ x/ x/ x/ x/ x/
x/ x/ x/ x/x

So many years are gone since first my heart in vain
    The goblet of King Jémshid wanted,
And so the treasure that the heart itself possessed
    It tried to find in other people—
It looked among the sad and sun-browned loving ones
    Who, crying, idled on the seashore:
It hoped to hold the pearl that in an oyster shell
    Was never seen, or long had vanished.
My problems yesterday had I confided to
    The kindly taverner, quite freely—
And he with care and trial finally had found
    An answer that would solve the riddle.
"I saw," he laughingly explained in teasing mood,
    "Within my hands, the wine-filled goblet"—
Behold the magic glass where he the mysteries
    In more than hundreds glimpsed, appearing.
I said to him: "O tell me, wise one, who revealed
    To you that perfect world-perspective?"
He said: "The Lord Creator, on the day when He
    From ore had forged the vault of heaven."
[He said: "One friend—his fate the gallows—had betrayed
    The Mystery—his only failing.
And if the Holy Spirit wish it, someone else
    Will give what the Messiah offered."]
He further said about the Lord: "He is the one
    Who raised aloft the might of rulers—
And He the one who in the bodied Universe
    The mysteries made clear and open.
The man aggrieved in heart had known not how the Lord
    About him hovered in his dwelling—
And so it had occurred, the God he couldn't see
    He felt—but only at a distance.
The fond illusions that the weaker Reason here
    Paraded first before our faces
Are like the trickeries the staff of mage Samír
    Displayed before the rod of Moses.

But any person whom the Angel Gabriel
        Has sent to aid him in his venture
Will be enabled to attain a wonderwork
        Much like the ones achieved by Jesus.
I asked the taverner: "Then tell me why the hair
        Of gentle Lady's like a fetter."
He said, "Your foolish heart, O Háfiz, to enchain!
        While others but lament and pity."

Reply

x/ x/ x/ x/ x/
x/ x/ x/ x/x

An allegory of the spirit-search
        (Though complicated) we're unveiling.
Sir Isaac Newton, too, had thought himself
        A little boy, upon the seashore,
Who'd now and then a "smoother pebble" found
        Or "prettier shell than ordinary,
Whilst the great Ocean" Truth, encompassing,
        Lay "undiscovered" all "before me."

Mansúr Al-Hállaj felt himself at one
        With darkest ocean-depth of Being.
"I am the Truth," he said, which also meant
        "I am the God," and shocked some hearers.
He met the gallows, and in quiet lines
        Interpolated (not in Hammer,
But which Wohlleben lends), the poet hints
        He told a mystic truth forbidden.

In scripture Allah said that we were made
        Of water (so are one with ocean):
The patience, pardon at the heart of things
        (Qur'anic phrase) I feel within me
When, open to the world beyond the shore
        And humbled, thinking now of Newton,
I look upon what's wider than the mind
        And bow before the Might Unspoken.

52. HÁFIZ-HAMMER I.220–21 DAL 10: DOSTAN DOCHTERĬ RES TÖBE SI MESTÙRI KERD

/xx /xx /xx /xx /

Friends! what a penance the vine's lovely daughter has done!—
Yes, with the watchman alert, her activities done.
Vine-Daughter purifies well, from the dripping of sweat,
Drinkers and says to them, Comfort!—your love's not undone.
Now is the time we delight in the cheer that she brings—
Long were the hours, lonely woe, when the damage was done.
Tidings of gladness, my heart! for the singer the air
Filled with a melody stirred with what fervor had done.
Don't be surprised that your breath had unbudded the hearts,
Hasn't the nightingale thus with the rose-garden done?
Sevenfold fire and a hundred times water—and yet
Wine-spot remains on the hood of the monk—not undone.
Meekness of *me* don't demand, for your enviers took
Faith, honor, wealth into darkness—ah, that's what they've done. . . .

Reply

Shuja, so Hammer explained, a great favor had done:
Wine-bans by earlier monarchs imposed he'd undone.
Greatly elated are tippler and toper today!
I, as a poet, my thinking have partly redone:
Nothing is harder than writing a Persian ghazal—
Once you've selected a word to repeat, what you've done
You will be stuck with, as here, till the Doomsday, or till
(After the test of your wit) your performance be done.
Like the jongleur, who's a minstrel and juggler at once,
You are a trickster of words, with your debt never done
Till you have shown to the public agility, skill,
Cleverly proving you cannot be baffled, undone.
Frankly, it's tough. Even Goethe, a poet of note,
Writing ghazals, felt relief when the project was done.

53. HÁFIZ-HAMMER I.240 DAL 22: GHULAMĬ NERKESĬ MESTĬ TU TADSCHDARANEND

/x /x /xx /xx /x

Masters—they're the slaves of your brilliant narcissi—
Ev'n the wise, excited and roused by your rubies—
Should the East-wind violets gently pass over,
Look what havoc envy among them is bringing!
You the wind betrays—I'm betrayed by my teardrops:
Never will the secret of lovers stay hidden.
I your rosy cheeks would belaud—yet surrender:
How compete with myriad nightingale-praises?
Smoothing out a hair-lock, then strokingly combing,
You will see, adhering, the otherwise faithless.
Paradise we surely in time will recover—
Who, if not we sinners, would merit the mercy?
Go to inns, and redden your face with their pleasure—
Visit not the cell where the hypocrite's brooding!
You, my fount of Khízer, be holy and help me:
I alone must walk, while the others are riding!
Never may our Háfiz be free of the tresses—
Only slaves of *you* may be counted the free ones.

Reply

Trochee, trochee, dactyl and dactyl and trochee.
Simple, right? And yet, were it really so easy
Such a pleasant metric invention to practice,
Why are lines like *these* never heard in our language?
Music, waken! You, who in Háfiz a freedom
Knew that rarely flourished in lands of our planet,
Come with caravanserai-wealth, and display it,
Tradesman-like, and make us aware of your wonders!
Lovers ruby-lipped and with eye-gleam narcissal
Charm the heart of Háfiz, the passionate dreamer.
I'm entranced when rhythm can set me a-dancing
Whether with the body or mind, or on paper.
Lyric lines are born from the spirit of music,
Lending life aesthetical justification:

He that makes a meter enlivening fingers'
Will to jump on keyboard, on rug of Aladdin,
Bears a higher grace in uplifting the spirit—
Higher far!—than Solomon, Tamerlane, Jémshid.

54. HÁFIZ-HAMMER I.242–43 DAL 24: SEMENBUJAN GHUBARĬ GHAM TSCHU BINISCHEND BINISCH ANEND

/x /x /xx /x
x/ x/ x/ x/x

Girls who wear a fragrance of jasmine
        May woe dispel when seated near you,
Maidens with their fairy-tale faces
        The calm will banish as they're leaving.
Look how these, with bond made of dolor,
        My wounded heart are binding softly,
Spicing hair with amber aroma
        They strew the way with souls that fainted.
Just one second—see how they vanish:
        Arrived—already, now, departing,
Rise and go: they've planted forever
        The longing-twig in hearts abandoned.
Now they laugh: the tears will be flowing
        Like agates on the cheeks of hearers:
Should my face be glimpsed for a moment
        My mystery will be detected.
Who may plumb the soul-perturbation
        Of loneliness will comprehend it—
Who the gleaming Friend-of-the-morning's
        Bright cheek will see, has known it early.
Many who consider the healing
        Of love a quick and easy effort
Find, with maidens seated about them,
        A hope of remedy elusive.
Beggars at the throne of the Mighty
        Begin their hymn with plaintive wailing:
Háfiz, when the throne he approaches,
        Will undergo a sorrow trial.

Reply

Trochees two, then double the dactyl,
        Quadruple trochee—Háfiz' meter.
How I love the calm and the canter:
        The maidens' coming, their departing,

Punctuate the pleasure with tension,
The rapid giving way to quiet.
I will breathe Hafizian meter
Repeatedly while growing older—
Wave-ascent, then lapsing and tranquil,
A framing of the mind's adventure.
Once begun, you feel the momentum
That doesn't want to break the pattern,
Halt the movement. Maybe I'd better,
However—I have made a "sonnet."

55. HÁFIZ-HAMMER I.310–11 DAL 72: DER ESEL PERTEVĪ HUSNET SI TEDSCHELLI DEM SED

/xx /xx /x /x
/xx /x /x /x
/x /xx /xx /x

When in eternity gleamed your beauty,
Born from reflections, Love arose, who
Then with flaming the universe livened.

Rays from your cheeks were an emanation:
Angels that viewed them were unresponsive!—
Vexed, resentful, She went to the people.

That's when the Intellect asked to have a
Spark to enkindle human beings.
Lightning Envy created the sparkle!

Loftier mysteries wanting, needing,
Rivals desired. A higher hand, though,
Kept the breast in a whirling confusion.

Fate that determines our lives would bring the
Luckiest love, for them appointed—
Me, a sorrowing heart and its worries.

Came the enheartening soul of worlds and
Hollowed a dimple, charming chin-mark—
Then it saved you by seizing your tresses.

That was the day that would take, O Háfiz,
Pleasures of love away forever,
Nothing left but perplexing dejection.

Reply

Fitting, the rhythm to one confounded—
Stumbling and ever searching, hurting—
Mired in muddle, the sunlight is hidden.

Hammer, however, a striking wisdom
Found that may offer sudden comfort:
What is Love, in Hafizian thinking?

Love's the reflection of primal beauty
Shining from *Her*, the Beloved, in the
State before the Creation, in Heaven.

There in the Realm of Ideas, where She
Dwelt in a blest, entire perfection,
See her—Mother of lights that are fallen.

Shadowed, absconded from those in matter—
Ray that preceded clay-encasing!
Why be plaintive and pained by the distance?

Háfiz, more lively than Cavalcanti
(That is the claim that Hammer's making),
Brought the moaner's dilemma before us

Not as a tragedy. Rather, Plato
Knows in the poet a Persian comrade:
Starlight shines in the eyes of the lover.

56. HÁFIZ-HAMMER I.322–23 DAL 80: HER KIRA BE CHATĬ SEBSET SEVDA BASCHED

x/ x/ x/
x/ x/ x/ x/x

Whoever once had felt
For gentlest down a vivid liking
Would never in his life
Again be stirring from your circle.
From dust of graves I rose
Burnt-centered as the tulip, branded,
To bear the sign-desire
Within me of your mark of beauty.
You, only pearl, reply!—
How long will you account it rightful
That eyes, because of you,
Be mourningly in flood forever?
May aromatic hair
Cast calmly on my head a shadow,
For only in the shade
Can my poor heart repose encounter!
From every eyelash flows
The tearful liquid forth in streamlets—
O Rose, approach, you love
Abiding by a shore well-watered.
And, like my heart, stay veiled,
The cover not one moment lifting—
I cannot feel assured
That ever I again will see you
For, out of pride, your eye
Has turned away from humble Háfiz:
The daffodil was glad
To let the sinking head bend lower.

Reply

(1)

Arisen from the tomb
Of one rejected, ever bearing
The central blackened brand

Of heart-consuming carmine ardor,
The tulip-troubadour
Of yearning ever unrequited
Will teach a lesson we
Cannot afford to hear unheeding:

Whom love does not defeat
Will be alone the one to pity.
Subjection to the best
Is martyrdom and therefore merit.
They die to live again
Whose only blame is adoration.
In every age, in praise,
Behold the tulip re-arising.

(2)
FOR ANDREI GURUIANU

The lines when read aloud
Will make the Persian ear imagine
A flute and barbiton
With gently tapping tabret mingled.

Who hasn't heard the tune
Will never know this lulling comfort
That smooths the brusque, abrupt,
With female rhythm we rely on.

The aphoristic mind
Will shape a gladly graven saying
Impressed upon the heart
Of one that will to carving hearken.

"Language reveals the man,"
Claimed Jonson. "Speak, that I may see thee."
Rhythm propels the mood,
Quaternal huing of the humors.

The heart will speak in beats
Nor kens another kind of language.
The hands will clap, a laugh
Accompanying summer psalmers.

The morrow—trust it!—brings
A newer shape of lover-strophe
With constellated lyre,
Unheralded configuration.

57. HÁFIZ-HAMMER I.327 DAL 83: DILĬ MA BEDEVRĬ RUJESCH SI TSCHEMEN FIRAGH DARED

/xx /xx /xx /xx /xx /x
/xx /xx / – /xx /xx /

Meadows my heart is evading—the face of the dear one has made me
 Cypress-like rooted in joy, tulip-like branded within.
Never before have I bowed my head down before gently curved eyebrows—
 I have a hermit become, saying goodbye to the world.
I am disturbed by the violet, tresses' aroma conveying:
 What had the dark one designed? what had been spun in the brain?
Shadows of night! and the terror of wilderness! what is your stature?
 See how the torch of the cheeks brightened the traveler's road!
Go to the meadow, and there have a look at the royal-throned rose-bloom:
 Tulips before her will stand, offering goblets prepared.
Hearts are you robbing, your radiant cheeks and your hair aromatic!—
 Thief never heard of before, stealing by fire-lighted day!
Háfiz but longs to become in the love-school an excellent pupil—
 Meadow and field he ignores, caring no more about these.

Reply

Lines brighter-hearted and lighter than most of the tulip-lamentings. . . .
 True, he had turned from the field, flower- and meadow-delight:
Yet there's a bit of good humor; he kept the hyperbole pleasant—
 Witty, the thought of a thief holding a torch to be seen.
Nothing so clearly reminds me of Goethe, in *West-Eastern Dívan,*
 Where, in a lyric, he comes, asking admittance to Heav'n,
Claiming as well, with temerity, martyrdom's qualification.
 When a receptionist asks, "Are you a martyr to faith?"
Goethe replies, in effect: "I am human, and therefore I struggled.
 Plus, being human, I loved—faith that is hard to maintain!
Everyone knows it will likely be doomed to a bleak disabusal:
 Yet I have guarded it well, martyr triumphant am I."
Goethe distinguished himself in the Sufi-Hafizian love-school:
 Tulip, be slave to the Rose—make it your homework today.

58. HÁFIZ-HAMMER I.358–59 POEM 105: MERAMEI DIGER BARE ES DEST BÜRD

/xx /xx /xx /xx /xx /x
/xx /xx / – /xx /xx /

Now has the wine yet again of the use of my faculties robbed me,
First, it dealt kindly, indeed—later it got me aroused.
Thousands of thanks to the wine, with its hue of the noblest of carmine,
Wiping away from my face all of the yellow of grief.
Gladly the hand I caressed that had first plucked the grapes which had helped me—
Favored may wander the foot active in treading them down.
Deeply impressed on the forehead, the lot by the fingers predestined—
Writing incised by that fate never will knife cut away.
Pray don't parade your philosophy now! At the hour when you're dying,
Baffled, defeated will be ev'n Aristoteles old!
Rather comportment maintain so that, watching the way you will follow,
No one will say when you die, "He will forever be dead."
Goblets of wine will excite every drinker by thoughts of uniting—
Lucky the lovers of wine, pure, that our Háfiz will drink.

Reply

Poet, I never stop thinking: in spite of your deep disputation,
You and philosophy won't *ever* stand wholly apart.
Beauty's unfolding the nature of one who in happy affirming
Grows like the oak that will spread branches benign over all,
Wisdom protecting their minds who, a poet-entelechy seeing,
Feel disposition become ample capacity wide.
Seed scatter trees, and the nightingales tone, and the rose an aroma—
Bard will, mellifluent, clothe Soul with the silks of the earth.
What is our Eden? A place where potential grows realization.
"Knowing yourself"—how's it done? Act, and become who you are.
Wine is an emblem of ardor, the sun-heat that drives the plant upward—
Thoughts of a union arise: I am united with Life.
May has arrived, and who fails to arrive at the same destination
Lags when he ought to be roused, grounded while nightingales fly.

59. HÁFIZ-HAMMER I.366–68 DAL 109: DUSCH DIDEM KI MELAIK DER MEICHANE SEDEND

/x /xx /x
/x /x /x

Angels worked in the tavern
(Yesterday, I swear it!);
Adam's clay were they pulping,
Pouring into goblets.

These attainers of highest
Purity and lordship
Glasses clinked with the drinker,
Me, the humble viewer.

Loving trust was a burden—
Heavens couldn't bear it.
I, a fool, was allotted
Thus the fated honor.

God be thanked that in concord
He and I are living—
Myriad houris have drunk a
Toast in wine, so grateful.

Keep my spirit away from
Many thousand errors!
One black seed in the Garden
Quite bewildered Adam.

Pray you, pardon the quarrel
Jarring sects enkindled;
Twelve-and-sixty contenders
Knew no truth, and blundered.

What may laugh in the candle?
Not authentic flaming.
Truer fire is the kind that
Burns the moth to ashes.

Love will carmine the hearts of
        Ardent corner-crouchers;
Thus the beauty-mark, fevered
        Cheek adorn the lover.

None like Háfiz removed the
        Veil from thought-expression
Since the locks of the word-bride
        Newly curled, were shining.

Reply

Scripture-wit is the topic:
        Háfiz loved allusion.
Swift, exuberant thinking
        Keeps tradition vivid.

First, the tale of creation
        Gained an added "spirit":
Angels knead in a wine vat
        Férment-clay of Adam.

Next, the gift of *amāna*,
        Trust divinely offered:
Creatures feared to accept it—
        All but Man, the bravest.

Here it's granted to Háfiz,
        Foolish, poor, unworthy.
Yet the comic reminder
        Lent the concept presence.

Houris drink to the honor
        Given to the poet,
Heaven-Muses applaud a
        Clever-witted singer.

Wheat seed, black, in the Garden
        (Eden-tale refashioned),
Now appears in a handsome
        Beauty-mark temptation.

Moth consumed in the candle,
    Bright, oneiric, fated
(Captivating to Goethe),
    Isn't quite Qur'anic,

Yet surrender to Allah—
    Breathing heart of Íslam—
Came alive in a wingéd
    Lyrical reframing.

So John Donne, in a Western
    Bold baroque rethinking,
Wrote his witty-religious
    Gift to old tradition.

60. HÁFIZ-HAMMER I.372–73 DAL 112: SCHIJU TER ENGISED CHATIR KI HASIN BASCHED

/xx /xx /xx /xx /xx /x
/xx /xx / – /xx /xx /

Might we expect that a gloom-laden mind take delight in our singing?
Well, let us try a few words, letting them be what they may.
Might I discover a ring that was made out of crimson-lipped rubies,
Hundredfold I would excel Solomon's realm in my wealth.
Calm, imperturbable stay, O my heart, when the enviers mock you—
Possibly, deeplier seen, something benign will be found.
When the perceiver can not comprehend my enlivening paintbrush,
He'll not be painting too well, be he from China—the best.
Heart-blood and wine were together for each of us humans predestined—
So, with encompassing range, fate had distributed lots.
Differing widely are destinies lent to the rosewater, roses.
Former you'll find being sold—latter in corner confined.
Ha! it can never occur that our Háfiz be cured of his drinking—
That is the gift of his fate—his to accept, not to change.

Reply

Striking the oddity here, and revealing of meaning implicit:
Contrasts in fate are his theme—yet, when examined, they fade.
Roses and rosewater: forms are contingent, admittedly differ—
Yet their idea: the same—sensory pleasure, and rare.
Heart-blood and wine, though contrastable, offer analogous features,
Heated in madness, or love—richened their redness in joy.
Quite understandable, then, that the classical dark Dionysus,
Dying, a seed, to arise—jinn of engendering, wild,
Mourned by the flutes' ulalú (in a mode reminiscent of Rumi),
God of the grape, would in wine lend the adherent a strength.
Jesus would later in dying the doctrine declare of his wine-blood—
He'd be adored as a god, too, in the rubious drink.
Háfiz, you've rightly perceived how the fates differentiate people—
Yet the examples you showed prove us more deeply the same.

61. HÁFIZ-HAMMER I.384–85 DAL 120: DIL BISUS KI SUSĬ TU KIARHA BÜKÜNED

/xx /x /x /
x/ x/ x/x

Kindle, my heart, the burning will
Avoid a slew of mischief,
Making the midnight keep away
A hundred kinds of evil.
Should you rebuke the handsome ones,
Employ the sweetest wording:
Kindly caressing eyes reproach
A hundredfold each roughness.
Whoso is liegeman of the glass
Wherein the world is mirrored
Surely will lift the hidden veil
That kept two worlds asunder.
Know that the physicker of love's
A fragrant-breathing savior.
Yet if he doesn't know you're ill,
Then whom would he be curing?
Trust to the Lord in all your deeds
And thus be joyful-hearted—
No one has pity on your lot?
The Lord will show you mercy.
Over my swift reverse of luck
I've reason to be grieving—
Yet may the One remember me
Upon the morning blessing.
Háfiz, morose!—aroma none
By friendly tresses wafted.
Still may the East-wind hint of *him*,
Restoring me to fortune.

Reply

Never a doubt that Allah will
The faithful soul be aiding,
Who at the dawning as at eve
The air finds blank and absent.

Gone from the tent the balmy trace
That evidenced a friendship.
Yet may a heaven-help be found
In morning-time devotion.
Reading the Daybreak Sura, pray
And feel a ray approaching.
God to the world aroma lent
Whereof the winds have spoken.
Fountains will gush in rocky waste,
Sad barren earth new-breathing.

62. HÁFIZ-HAMMER I.429–30 DAL 93: BER SAÌ BASARĬ DSCHAUBASAN MUNADÌ MISENEND

/xx /xx /xx /xx /xx /x
/xx /xx /, /xx /xx /

Listen!—for what is the call from the merchant of souls at the market?
Hark to the region of souls, hear the inhabitants there.
Days have already gone by since the vine's lovely daughter went missing—
Hold her importance in mind: open your eyes, look around!
Ruby of hue was her dress, and her crown as the foam of the ocean—
Lately gone out of her mind, she will be needing your aid.
Anyone who can deliver the bitter, with sweet be rewarded!
Even if hell hold her fast, seize her, return her to me.
Bitter and sharp and most heady at night is the rosy-hued maiden,
Soon as you find her, come quick! Bring her to Háfiz's room.

Reply

Omar Khayyám had informed us the barren old helpmeet of Reason
He had divorced from his bed, roistering rather with Joy.
It was the vine's lovely daughter, the same that enchanted our Háfiz,
Came to the room of the bard, mathematician and mage.
Wine, with her madness and bitterness—why would I eagerly seek her?
Wishing to amplify bliss, nightingale-brave will I sing.
Words in Ovidian rhythm can aid me, but afterwards adding
Strings to the heat of the heart, I will a chorister be
Joining the birds of the forest, indeed with a tree-spirit playing:
Silent in life, she becomes, now, in her sleep, violin.

63. HÁFIZ-HAMMER II.19 RA 11:
DIGER SI SCHACHĬ SERVSEHI BÜLBÜLĬ SABUR

/xx /xx /xx /xx /xx /x
/xx /xx /, /xx /xx /

Hear how the nightingale's chanting again from the bough of the cypress—
Far be the evil-eye harm, far from the face of the rose!
Rose, being grateful that you are the sultaness, monarch of beauty,
Show yourself never too proud, hearing the nightingale-plaint.
I will in patience refrain from lamenting your distance in lyric:
Who separation is spared, happy return cannot know.
Oh, how the pious for palace and houris in Eden are hoping!
I have a castle and friend here in the tavern beneath.
Drink up your wine to the tune of the lute—if the meddlesome tell you
Wine is forbidden, reply: God is the Pardoning One!
Others in joy and fresh air find the spring of a cheerful demeanor—
Sorrow of love is, for me, source of all air and all joy.
Tell me then, Háfiz, what use in lamenting a long separation?
Out of the darkness, the light—hard isolation, then bliss.

Reply

Happy the man with perpetual faith in reliable pardon!
See him forgiving the fair comrade, and thinking the best.
Wine's a preventive purgation for blaming, arisen from sadness.
Roses are quiet, and yet nightingales poems compose.
Lyric and fragrance are breathed in a genial and generous lending:
Better to give than receive—teaching of blossom and bird.
He of the night is an emblem, the psalmer of Allah in darkness—
Rose an awareness had brought, doubly: aroma'd and bright.
Words are unneeded by twofold arousing of nature and beauty—
Only the cynical find sorrow in welling-up life.
Háfiz, forgiving himself in a mood only few will find puzzling,
Knows the reward of the hour, kissing the moment that flies.
Time and the mind are espoused in the house of a lordlier heaven
Fit for the poet and one who in the morning will bloom.

64. HÁFIZ-HAMMER II.32 SA 3:
CHOSEH AN SCHEBI KI DERAJI BESAD GIRISCHME VÛ NAS

/x x/ x/ x/ x/x
x/ x/
x/ x/ x/ x/x
/x x/ x/ x/ x/x
x/ x/
x/ x/ x/ x/x

Blessed the night! when you with your enchantment
Have come to me,
When you caress, to my imploring.
Look! to the east a secret I'm confiding;
How *can* the bud
In springtime yet remain unopened?

High is my fortune, merely now awaiting
Your fuller growth;
Your hair—I wish it years of living:
Fate, what an uproar you have raised, adorning
It graciously
With wide narcissus-eye bright-shining.

Ha! what a ringing made I at the heart-gate,
The entry bell—
Throughout the night with fevered longing.
Shall I regard a rival's grief and think of
That plaintive woe?
The slave of love must bear great sorrow.

Often when Rose will laugh the eastern spirit
Will lend repose—
To blabbermouth may God be kindly!
Dust of an ardor blinds a rival vision—
To dust incline
Your forehead, Háfiz, be contented.

Reply

(1)

Poets may love to write of blushing roses,
        But here alone
    The heat that smoldered in the whiteness
Borne by the glory-wind-aroma'd morning
        Conveyed to me
    A fragile, tender maiden breathing.

Choiring, the bird outside, and brimming over!
        The palest frame
    The tender carmine of the center
Folding, and I, when early dew refreshes,
        Together make
    Aubade, afar, to greet you, fair one.

Light of the inner glow, unfurling, speaking
        Of Allah-Dawn
    And of His law that we may wildly
Dwell on a whirling planet flaming, turning,
        I bow to you,
    Revere a fragrant, holy token.

He that infusing into Háfiz, Rumi
        A will to hymn
    Had smiled on garden-drunken dancer
Telling in tone and quiet of the pulsing
        In bloom and blood—
    My thankful canticle completed.

(2)

Love for the nightingale, the rose, the drunken
        Still darkling cure
    That Persian Háfiz turned to versing
Told me that life may be a will to lyric
        And halfway there
    Already in the grateful dreamer.

Myriad-clear the story-morphing music
That heard the pulse,
The Primal Mover, heart-empowered,
Known as the Tetragrammaton-surrender,
As Love alone—
Buraq I see again ascending.

Feathers within the wings of Michael highest
On Lote-Tree bough
Are each an emerald—all flying
Higher by far in sight, a thrust, an impulse.
Our trust and hope
Are one. Let energy engender

Here, in my anthems, You that in the many
Will psalm-lines write,
A greening hymn and crimson singing,
Azuring amplitude and purple mind-whirl
That whoso hears
May shout with Rumi, clap with Háfiz.

(3)

Beautiful Vestal weather might be whether
More fitly styled
For them that love a sense of drama:
Mountain-goat climate whimsied, apt for caper—
From day to night
The drop can seem a change of season.

Here is a bird of simple two-note musing,
Discordant crow
To answer, minor third repeated.
Chill is the autumn rawness, yet augmentor
Of inner heat,
The widened lung imbibing vigor.

Younger the blood becomes, O mentor-master!
Of poet-craft
A pioneer I call you, lauding.
Teaching a Grecian freedom, Persian humor,
In German tune,
You came to aid both me and Goethe.

Rhythm of lyric sixty-four by Háfiz,
My cup I raise
To you in this eternal moment!
Hammer, conclamant in our dithyrambing,
Your hallowed name
We hymn at daybreak and in thunder.

(4)
Magic Rose
A TRUE-LIFE STORY TOLD BY SHAHID ALAM

Ámena'd been perplexed a bit, and worried:
The teacher seemed
Inclined to quite annoying rigor.
Judged from the sample lesson (unappealing!)
Could he impart
Piano skill—and she enjoy it?

Ámena's ten. I like her. Very clever.
You'd right away
Exclaim, on hearing her, What talent!
Hearing her father speak, I wondered whether
The teacher'd been
Let go, the coming visit canceled. . . .

"What can we do?" she asked. Her father pondered:
"I think I know
The answer, for a rose contains a
Magical way of making people over."
They bought a bloom.
Each petal spread aroma'd welcome.

So, when the teacher came, to him she handed
The flow'r and said,
"A gift." That hardened spirit melted,
Gentle was every word he spoke thereafter
Who, startled, moved,
Responded, "Never in my lifetime—

Never did such a thing occur. Amazing."
        I sing of this
    In rhythmic strophe new-imbibed from
Háfiz in Joseph Hammer's bülbül chanting.
        In Shíraz we
    Espy, today, the magic roses.

65. HÁFIZ-HAMMER II.81–82 SCHIN 18: HATEFI ES KÖSCHEI MEILHA NE DUSCH

/xx /xx /xx /x

Someone not seen, in a nook of the tavern,
Yesterday said, "Well, drink up, you'll be pardoned.
Allah's forgiveness is readily granted,
Angels proclaiming the grace and good tidings.
Effort and stress are no helpers of pleasure—
Heart, make an end to the tension oppressive!
Ear-charm of hair from the comrade will suit you—
Dust from the tavern the face is befitting.
Férment of mind is no mortal transgression—
Háfiz may think of the shah and his mildness,
Shuja the faithful, the generous—even
Gabriel, who is an angel, paid homage."
King of the Heaven! Extend to him blessing,
No evil eye come to trouble our monarch!

Reply

Justification in galloping dactyl,
Happily wedding the form to the content,
Feels like a ride on a horse through the country,
Gaining in tempo while spirits are lightened:
After a moment, so rapid the canter,
Well may we feel on a current transported,
Body of steed into ether dissolving,
Lightning-Buraq rising up to the heaven,
Quick to compete with a meteor, comet—
Leaving the sphere of the star of the evening,
Zohra, the fourth, where the breathing of Jesus
Healing effuses with dewlike devotion—
Nearing the Garden, approaching the Lote-Tree,
Brightened by emerald shining of Michael.

66. HÁFIZ-HAMMER II.94 DHAD 1: HUSNU DSCHEMALĬ TU DSCHIHAN DSCHÜMLE GIRÜFT TULU ARDH

x/ x/ x/ xx/ x/
x/ x/ x/ xx/ x/
x/ x/ x/ x/x
/xx /xx /x /x

The sweet alluring charm of your face had seized
The ravished world in all of its length and breadth:
The sun of heaven is embarrassed
Now by the lunar competing beauty.

To me it seems but fitting that everyone
Should treasure that attractiveness here below—
Your countenance bedecked in splendor
Angels above may regard in homage.

The sun must borrow light in his sphere (the fourth)
From luster of your cheeks that refulgent gleam:
She, modest, hides in shame—the seventh,
Lowest, of earths were the proper dwelling.

The spirit holding back adoration must
Inanimate remain, and for evermore—
Dispelled and scattered be the bodies
Coldly unwilling enslaved to aid you.

For you, O Háfiz, 'twere but an idle act
To kiss the dust of earth at the feet of her—
The raving tale of all your longing
Told by the clamoring winds about you.

Reply

If sapphic music moves in a stately flow—
Asclepiadic, zigzagging to and fro—
Alcaic will the spirit nourish,
Building to forcibly stormy flourish.

Of all the ancient meters I yet have found
Alcaic rhythm, brisker than any sound
    The Greeks have lent, induces wonder:
        Vernal and freshening—rain and thunder!

The first two lines, containing a dactyl each,
Move quickly, then the smoothening third will teach
    A quiet waiting. All the greater
        Flare of the trumpet a moment later!

67. HÁFIZ-HAMMER II.106–107 AIN 4: DER WEFAI ISCHKI TU MESCHHURĬ CHOBANEM TSCHU SCHEMIJ

x/ x/ x/ x/ x/ x/x

'Mid handsome ones I'm famous, faithful as the candle—
I sit at night amid the drunken, like the candle.
By night or day no sleep my weary eyes will favor—
I'm weeping, sick with separation, as the candle.
The shears of grief have snipped my fraying thread of patience—
Yet in the heat-glow of your love I laugh, a candle.
Send butterfly Desire amid the night of rending,
Or I might set the world on fire, like any candle!
If bloody tears weren't streaming from my eyes in quiet,
There's no one who would see my spirit, like the candle.
My weeping heart, you see it caught, 'twixt heat and water?
It never ceases to lament, a plaintive candle.
The rock of patience molten down like wax from grieving
Can prove my life with love is melting like the candle.
My day is dark without your world-illuming beauty,
Yet incomplete and self-dissolved is love, a candle.
Your flame of blazing love has captivated Háfiz:
But when will water quench this burning of a candle?

Reply

My little daughter once, when looking at a candle,
Began to cry; she feared the dying of the candle.
I hope I never will forget the tender moment:
We cry to see light go—our life is but a candle.
Yet feel the minute—so transcending in its beauty!—
'Twill climb above the little limit of the candle.

And it is not a wonder, that amid the weeping,
And even rage, as of a conflagration-candle,
The poet, smiling at enkindling by the lover,
Can laugh in ample triumph, as an avid candle!—
An angry, smiling, weeping, laughing human being,
A dying-living soul envisioned in a candle.

Our fortune is a freedom, ev'n when borne in sorrow,
A centered energy, an eye-requiting candle.
The cheerful splendor Hegel viewed in Háfiz' writing
Made clear entirely in the image of a candle,
The many colors in the flaming eye concentered
Alembicating into light the waxen candle.

68. HÁFIZ-HAMMER II.118–19, KAF 1: MAKAMĬ ENNU BIGHASCH VE REFIKĬ SCHEFIK

/xx/, /xx/, /xx/
x/ x/ x/ x/ x/ x/x

Place that is safe, wine that is pure, friend that is true,
And these the three that you've been granted, fate delightful!
Truths of the world, deeds of the world, all are in vain;
A thousand times have I confirmed that rule of merit.

Quickly to find safety at last—limited time!—
For robbers lurking in the rearguard lie awaiting.
Sad and alas! up till today never I'd known
The one I chose for guide would lead to lucky fortune.

Over the cup, rubious wine, penance to do
Is merely phantom-thought—the reason won't support it.
Chin-dimple fine! This will contain loveable charm
No rich and myriad wisdom ever can encompass!

Where is my heart?—leading me wise, onto the path:
My friend I never could succeed, astray, in finding.
Slender the waist—wonder to see—even if I
May no embrace attain, the mind will take its pleasure.

Ruby recall, mentioned before—why be surprised?
The eye an ardent pyrope for a ring will offer.
Smiling the mouth: Truly I'm yours, never a doubt. . . .
O Háfiz! like a little boy he'll fool and lead you!

Reply

(1)

Tune up the flute, string up the harp, strike up the band!
And grab your partner by the hand, and next encircle
Gently her waist, whirl her about, then to embrace
Will after all the dancing be the pretty sequel.

Never before, traveling bard, seeking delight,
Have you, the motley minstrel, rhapsodizing wildly,
Dared to perform, free of constraint, willing as wind,
A more entrancing folk-dance over plain and meadow.

Follow the sun, tracing the brook, fording the stream,
And bring a picnic lunch, and spread it on the greensward.
Louder the heart, warmer the blood, higher the mind—
We follow Háfiz to the promised land of pleasure.

(2)

Quaffing the wine, singing a hymn, thanking the Lord,
A poet, comforting on dusty earthly journey,
Slumbering vine waking acclaimed, bidding the man
Rewarded be in sweet rejuvenating virtue.
Prospering palm sheltering all, rubious fruit
Who eat and drink in shadow while the sun is climbing
Echo the law saying to those baffled and dry
That spirit by enjoyment grows in holy making.
Tabret and flute, barbiton bold, zither and lute
Enhance the fervor of the dancing of the dervish:
Rhythm to play, altering soon, moves with a mood
That like the streaming heaven-cloud will shape be shifting.
Music and wine, dancing and chant, psalming in awe
Enable widened heart to make the Great Surrender.

Even the Lord, let us recall, Being complete,
Could not endure to bear a unity unsundered:
Better create, God would decide, creaturely life
That One might mean more deeply when a Two were blended.
Gratified love came when the eye mirrored the glance
That flowerlike affirmed the ardor of the Garden:
Friends will convert languor to health, drowsy to rouse,
That each might aid the other in their skyward climbing.
Mortal are we, nor can attain knowledge in love
Except when goaded by a delegate to help us,
Messenger lent, heralding birth, life to beget
With energy reflected, willing eyes enkindled.
Thus when a friend, lover you have, angels appear
To bid you write and sing and paint and dance, embracing.

69. HÁFIZ-HAMMER II.139 LAM 6: EI BÜRDE DILEMRA TU BEDIN SCHEKL U SCHAMAIL

x/ x/ x/ x/ x/ x/

You stole away my heart with mantic, magic pow'r,
There's no one whom you fear, the world belongs to you.
I pull from out my heart a sigh, and then a dart—
And how to tell you what my soul has undergone?

The rubies of your lips—how laud before the foe?
The fools will never prize the richly colored wares.
The beauty of your might so grows from day to day
The moon can not confront you but withdraws in shame.

You stole my heart—to you my soul I gladly gave,
And freely—what collector ever need come by?
You in love's harem trod your Háfiz underfoot—
Embrace my garment hem, and other men's deny.

Reply

The alexandrine that expands in Baudelaire
And Pushkin and Mickiewicz in a majesty
To sweep with noble amplitude porphýrogene
Authority to lover-moan had stately lent.

The moon is overruled and power is our theme:
With love as weaponry, and beauty—blazoned crest,
The lady is implored in royal overture
Whose drum and trumpet-flourish magnify the might.

Thus love and worship in a courtly anthem can
With dolor merge when planished in an olden frame,
A reverential plaint in hymn-humility
Bow happily before the presence of the One.

70. HÁFIZ-HAMMER II.170–71 MIM 14: TA SAJEĬ MUBAREKET UFLADE BER SEREM

x/ x/ x/ x/ x/

So long as on my head your shadow falls
I'll be your servant, thrall to happiness.
Full many a year I never knew such luck,
Yet you that pleasure brought to me at last—
There's no one in the world will see me wake
When I have seen your image come in dream.
I live unendingly with pain of you—
Without you, though, no minute can I live.
No doctor kens a way to quell my grief,
My malady or health my friend will make.
You warned, Don't dawdle in my part of town,
And yet because of you I cannot leave.
All people serve the Shah and the Vizier.
O Háfiz—littlest of the Sultan-thralls!

Reply

"Adore" is *ad-orare*, that's "to pray,"
And paying "homage" means "I am your man."
Religion, love both focus on the one
To whom devotion tells: the goal is found.
The couplets are a double, but they form,
Each one, a single thought and all the same.
Antiphonal, the litany revealed,
Responsively involved, a sponsal rite.
The body-mind, while breathing out and in,
Beloved world could show that filled the heart—
For love will alter everything we live
And turn it to a gratitude for life.
Repetitive the sentiment?—no more
Than repetitious were my very breath.

71. HÁFIZ-HAMMER II.223 MIM 43: SEREM MOCHESTVE BEBANGĬ PÜLEND MIGOJEM

x/x x/x x/x x/
x/x x/x x/x x/x

Light-minded, excited, I'll say it quite loud:
I'm seeking in goblets a life-joy that's breathing.
The drinkers don't merit the scorn of the monk—
A pupil of drinkers of wine-dregs, I'm gladdened.
If doors of the tavern aren't open to me,
Then where should I knock, and where else find a helper?
Don't mock me for being self-raised, little trained—
Wherever's the nourishment, that's where I flourish.
Of mosque and of taverns don't speak to me, please—
As God is my witness, where *He* is, there *I* am.
The dust will become the philosopher's stone,
And I'll be the slave of the dust-balm of amber.
With love for the charming narcissus I'm filled—
A tulip, I wait on the bank of the river.
Confused by refusal, I'm famous afar,
A polo-ball trapped in the net of the tresses.
Bring wine! be the fatwa of Háfiz observed,
From dust of hypocrisy cleaning the spirit!

Reply

I think of the dust, and the grasses of Whitman,
The scorn of the spotless, the comrade besought,
The feeling of God on the road where you travel,
The ethic of joy in the world as it stands.
They're scruffy and rough and outsiders, but happy
In friendship extended and eager to praise.
Our lives being brief, we have need to acknowledge
The brave who the burden of living accept
And love without questioning, confident always
That God in our sandals can walk on the earth.

72. HÁFIZ-HAMMER II.225 MIM 45: RUSI IDEST VE MEN IMRUS DER AN TEDBIREN

/xx /x /xx /x
/xx /x /xx /x

Now is the time for planning the thirty
Days of the fast—I'm spending them drinking.
Several days I haven't seen glasses,
Cupbearer, wine—there's much that is lacking.
Ha! I would flee from cell-life reclusive
Even if monks a fetter had fastened.
Preachers a healing counsel have offered—
I, though, rejected every advisor.
Where is the guide that dies in the tavern,
So, at his feet, I also might perish?
Look, I am drunken, here, with the carpet—
Woe! when the folk the fake are disclosing.
Háfiz, the people say the familiar
Wine is worth more than hundreds of oldsters.

Reply

Perfect the beat in triple and duple
Syllable feet, for making a sonnet.
Fluting will change in lyric unwearied,
Moving renewed in winsomer whimsy.
Preacher and monk and hundreds of geezers
Calm have achieved—but paying with boredom.
Who is the fake, and who the authentic?
Drinkers, at least, are holding the moment.
Who would imprison heat and the wisdom
Fever may pour in fantasy-longing?
Folk go to work—for whom are they working?
You are the soul, the only employer!
Youth to return, some wine is sufficient:
Ardor of heart—undrying, undying.

73. HÁFIZ-HAMMER II.229–30 MIM 48: ASCHIKĬ RUĬ DSCHOVANĬ NEV CHASTE EM

x/ x/ x/ x/x x/
x/x x/ x/ x/ x/x

A fresh-faced youth—with him, I've fallen in love:
From God I obtained, by praying, this affliction.
Enchanted, deep in love, I cry it aloud—
That you, from my words, may comprehend my virtue.

Ashamed am I of wine, bespotted with wine—
With cunning, deceit, I patched the cowl, repaired it.
O candle! gently burn before him in woe,
This duty have I, myself, now undertaken.

Amazing how, from me, all profit had fled—
In pain had I won what from the spirit vanished.
In hope the fresh-faced youth may hug me, perhaps,
Today, as would Háfiz, I will haunt the taverns.

Reply

Equivocal the virtue—wouldn't you say?—
That made of the shame alone a signal merit.
The more we read of Háfiz, hearing the woe,
The more we will likely find our feelings riven.

The candor of the man, uncommon indeed—
Confession of weakness—may a sympathetic
Response attain, a sadness known to the Bard
Who pictured a Falstaff, libertine and réject.

A clever game, to juggle character roles:
Is Háfiz in hiding? Is the lover Háfiz?
Or is the poet here divided in two?
And what are the implications of the drama?

74. HÁFIZ-HAMMER II.231–32 MIM 50: TA SEH MIGUJEM VE ES GUFTEĬ CHOD DIL SCHADEM

/xx /xx /xx /xx /xx /x
/xx /xx /, /xx /xx /

First I will tell it out loud, with the greatest of joy in the telling:
I am the servant of love, free both in life and in death.
I am the bird of a world more supernal—I cannot explain it—
How I abruptly fell down, suddenly, into this net.
Formerly I was an angel and dwelt up above in the heaven—
Then to the wilds I was led—old Father Adam at fault.
Ah, but the paradise tree, and the Sélsebil spring, and the houris—
All of them long I'd forgot, simply in thinking of you.
Still is my fate undiscovered by all astrological knowledge—
Answer me, Lord, when I ask: what am I destined to be?
I, when a servant, devoted, the tavern of love was frequénting,
Nothing but burdens anew daily a visit would bring.
Heart-blood had reddened my eyes—and my wildness the least of my worries:
Fool to surrender my heart!—why did I give it to *them*?
Writ on its tablet is only the "one" of my Friend, letter *álif*—
That's what my Master had taught—nothing more wise could I know!
Drying my manuscript lines with the ends of your beautiful tresses:
Don't let the tear-flowing soak shelter from Háfiz away.

Reply

(I)

Free though a servant—a bird in the spheres of the lower and higher,
Only the "A" of the "one," Alpha, is writ in the heart.
Doctrine Platonic—if this in the lines of the Persian we're wanting,
Here is a myth-laden place. Weeping, yet dowered with wings,
Angel new-fallen, the memory weak, Eden only illumined
Briefly by one who arose bright anamnesis to lend,
Telling of something supernal that never a scryer envisioned:
Háfiz, or Adam, or Man, earth torn away from the Sun.
"One" in the heart, the inscription that never may wane or be faded,
Tells of the many as well, abecedarian ray.

Light being sown in the soul, can it flourish in courts of the Daybreak?—
    Cedar and cypress alike, towering up to the Eye.
Thus will the allegorizer be comforted, weary of seeking—
    Lately unriddled the fate writ in the form of the stars.

(2)
SYMPOSION

I raise the veil that separates
The upper, nether realm—I scant
No hospitality, decant
The wine that will unite our fates.

The fowler found not in the snare
The fledgling that from Lote-Tree fell,
And he can yet remember well,
The blazing em'rald angel there.

The ardent wine is not more red
Than heated blood in lover's heart,
Nor shall the ire of Iblis' art
Dim fire the *álif* sign had fed.

Alive, the dead can travel and
Will share the cup of company.
You, starlike Háfiz, are to me
The eye upon my *hamsa* hand.

75. HÁFIZ-HAMMER II.283–84 NUN 5: TSCHENDANKI GÜFTEM GHAM BETABIBAN

x/ xx/ xx/ xx/
x/ xx/ xx/

As much as to doctors my woe I've bewailed,
The sufferer's never been healed.
The love-pearl is gone from the long-coldened ring—
Let enviers, too, feel bereft.
O say to the thorn-rounded rose: "Are you not
Ashamed when the nightingale sings?"
I'm praying to God that to lovers he give
The sight of the face of the loved.
To all of my friends I've complained of my pain—
Who heals when the doctors are ill?
O revelers all at the table of treats,
My burden how long must I bear?
No more would your Háfiz be mocked by the world
If only some cure he might learn.

Reply

O Háfiz, your troubles are worse than I thought,
For blindness defied them in vain.
If all of your love is but doomed to defeat,
Are sorrows not lessened when shared?
Yet words, idle words are the least of your needs—
I'll honor you more, and be still.

76. HÁFIZ-HAMMER II. 297–98 NUN 16: SCHAHĬ SCHIMSCHAD KADDAN CHOSRU SCHIRIN DEHENAN

x/ x/ x/
x/ x/ x/
x/ x/ x/ x/ x/x

The shah of slender men,
The lord of honeyed bards,
Who with an eyelash every heart is whipping
(And so he wandered drunk)
Had just now glanced at me
And said: "You eye and lamp of those well-spoken,
Your purse, of silver, gold
How long has empty lain?
Become my slave and love the silver-bodied!
More slight than mote in sun,
Lose neither love nor lust,
But upward whirl as to the heav'n ascending.
The world holds no support—
You have a glass of wine:
Bring *this* to those of forehead fair and lovely."
My tavern-comrade, though
(All mercy on his soul),
Stepped in: "Beware of all the oath-betrayers!"
The eastern wind I asked,
"On tulip-richened sward,
What martyr witness all the carmine tomb-cloths?"
It answered: "Háfiz, we
Were not the secret lent.
Then chant the ruby wine, the sweet-lipped maiden!
Hold friendly garment-hem
And lend no thought to foes—
Be God's own man and never fear the devil."

Reply

The shabby tavern crowd
Can be a loutish lot:
'Tis hard to tell the sinner from the Sinner.

An old, besotted friend
May be a means of grace,
A drunk, inveterate, and yet a rescue.
I love it that the wind
Upon an eastern mead
Can hold a spirit-serving tone attentive—
The tulips, Háfiz, pure
As any breath of May,
Have heart of crimson, martyr-phantom vanished.

77. HÁFIZ-HAMMER II.387 JA 21: BE FIRAGHĬ DIL SEMANÌ NASAR BEMAHRUJI

x/ x/ x/ x/ x/x
x/ x/ x/ x/ x/

To gaze on moon-bright face with mind unhindered
Is better than high lordship's rush and roar.
And I'm in envy of the eyes. They're favored,
Unfairly, with the right to look on you.
My heart is lost, I know not where it wandered—
My life is gone as well, still more unknown.
And now my final breath has come—can't see you!
Although that was the only thing I'd wished.
East-wind, don't stir the hairs, the Péri-gentle;
To these had Háfiz guided myriad souls.

Reply

The eyes might well be envied!—never burdened
With later guilt, they look at what they like.
The heart, the life, the final breath are punished—
A tripled scapegoat, unremitted sin.
Blind Oedipus might of an eye be jealous
That innocently looked and didn't act.
Was Augustinus envying the manhood
That moved indifferent to Reason's will?—
A body part the theologic thinker
For insubordination had condemned.
A man in a Gogolian novella
His roguish Nose had envied, who'd attained
A more prestigious governmental function
Than ev'n the hero dreamed of or desired.
The eye, the nose, or any wayward organ
You like—blame *that*, and you'll improve your mood.

78. HÁFIZ-HAMMER II.400–401 JA 30: DU JARĬ SIREK U ES BADEI KÖHEN DÜMENI

x/x x/x x/x x/

Two jovial friends and two buckets of wine,
Some leisure, a book, and a corner secure
Are more than the world or the afterlife worth,
Though hordes of reproachers are eager to scold.
Whoever surrenders that corner of peace
Sells Joseph in Egypt for nothing at all.
Come in! there is plenty of room to include
The pious like you, and the sinner like me.
In time of affliction confide in the wine,
There's no one so faithful in eras like ours.
Be still in the corner—consider the thing:
Whoever had dreamèd such a dreadful dispute?
My name has been soiled in the hands of the low:
So heaven rewarded my trustworthy work.
O heart, remain patient—your rescuer, God,
A Solomon-ring will restore from the jinn.
The storms of the age make it hard to divine
If jasmine or rose in the garden survive.
O wonder! disclosed by the blowing simoom,
The jasmine and rose aromatic appear!
O Háfiz! the world's gone to ruin indeed;
And where is the Brahman physician to heal?

Reply

So pleasant to think of the quiet at home,
To read in the corner and speak with a friend—
Were Abu Huraira perusing my tune,
He'd add that a cat would the picture complete—
Though Háfiz, who's doubled his bucket of wine,
More cats might imagine than Shíraz can hold.
Political conflict, whatever the source,
Has fall'n with affliction on citizens all—
Full many a jasmine- and rose-bloom are gone
(Poetical gentling of hardship more harsh).
The poet is hopeful despite the despair

That lately arose when it seemed that the ring
Of Solomon, stolen from Órmuzd the Good,
Turned now irretrievably Áhriman-gain.
Whenever the spirit of evil can seize
The ring of the monarch, beware the result!
The fate that had frowned on the city at large
A smile to a few has accorded in love.
But stories of Bídpai, the Indian sage,
Past image of wisdom, the Brahman, present—
Regrettably lacking, for all we can do,
In these ineluctably violent times.

79. HÁFIZ-HAMMER II.410–11 JA 36: SI DILBEREM KI RESANED NU VASISCHĬ KALAMÌ

/xx /xx /xx /xx /xx /x
/xx /xx /, /xx /xx /

Where is the East-wind, the herald, the one whom I gladly would honor,
Would he but bring from the friend, treasured, a letter of hope!
No, I don't want to complain, but the comrade not yet in his kindness
Moistening longed-for has brought—thirsty and parched is the heart.
What, in the way of the lover, can reason be aptly compared to?
It is a droplet of dew, sunk in the deep of the sea.
Come! for my cowl will make clear that the tavern's my charity poorhouse—
Only one difference behold: never a penny I get!
Why don't the friends buy a sugar cane reed for the sweeter of speakers,
Who with a melody-quill plenty of honey could pour!
Now is my heart in an uproar—the tabret and habit perturb me.
I a new standard would plant, right at the door of the pub.
Little the wandering doctor may know of the trouble of lovers;
You, who have died, look about!—healer with Jesus-breath seek!
How, though, and where?—the confusion!—I'm rapidly getting a headache. . . .
Drink from the goblet, and feel one or two minutes of rest.
Come! for a clear understanding will show that the earth and the heaven
Less than a goblet will mean, sweetened by intimate talk.
Joying and reveling ever is not what a lover's awaiting—
Those who know well of our ways plenty of sorrow will drink.
Háfiz no trait will possess to attract one so lofty and slender—
Nothing but greeting at eve, nothing but prayer at dawn.

Reply

How to relate to a singer like this, wine-enslaved, love-abandoned?
Easily!—readers will know sorrow inherent in life.
Even in woe he remembered the lines that had won him affection:
Wealth he may never acquire—yet is he loved for his gift.
I am not wasted by loneliness, nor do I visit a tavern—
Yet, with my melody-drive, "Háfiz, be grateful!" I say.
No one is writing the intricate tunes in Ovidian distichs
Or in the rhythm we hear, blood-rousing, radiant, strange,
Found in the wonder-rendition of Háfiz by Joseph von Hammer—
No one, I say, but myself. "Who is the lonely?" I ask.

Only the fact that a colleague will read what I'm chanting and love it,
    Only the ones who, I know, like what will rise in the heart,
Only the kindness they show in responding with dialogue-answers,
    Only because they maintain spirit to relish a song—
Solely by cordial support from the reader who's willing to hear me
    Hymning in ways that revive souls of the poets of old
Life can be furthered by one who's at home in the versing of Persia:
    Friends are the Solomon-ring lending command of the heart.
Háfiz and Hammer have caught it—the meaning of greeting at evening,
    As of the prayer at dawn—'tis but my trust in a friend.
Daily the houris that come to the singer with quill-tip well-honeyed
    Love in the heaven confirm: write! the divine one may hear.

80. HÁFIZ-HAMMER II.413–14 POEM 38: SI KUI JAR MI A JED NESIMĬ BADĬ NEV RUS

x/ x/ x/ x/ x/ x/x

The timely festal breath has come from Comrade's region—
Enkindle then, if you would like, the waiting heart-lamp.
Have *you*, as do the roses, gold? On love expend it!
Karún the rich, by gold abandoned, lay in ruin.
But I've the purest wine, though pious minds decry it:
O Heaven! let the wise be free of every evil!
If you'd attain your wish, then practice self-denial—
Your freedom-shelter will consist in will-transcending.
I know not what the creekside turtledove is cooing—
Perhaps like me she spends her day and night in sorrow.
Your comrade sweet has flown—then be alone, O candle!
For that's your fate—remaining patient, burning purely.
I say a hidden thing: come forth, resemble roses!
But solely to admire, bereft—that is forbidden.
Come, Taverner! the hypocrite's a fool forever.
Drink wine, rouse up, O heart! and disregard the carpers.
I'd startled be indeed if you knew something better.
To meadows go, and from the nightingale learn loving—
Come join our friendly group, and learn the songs of Háfiz.

Reply

How often is the "alexandrine," with a lordly
Distinction come from one who conquered all of Asia,
Perceived to be a form appropriate for topics
And moods of mastery—yet here we feel it flowing
More smoothly than the winding movement of Meander.
When self-renunciation is the chosen topic
'Tis fit to imitate a peaceful-rhythmed breathing
With moan of turtledoves in immemorial elm-trees.
(I take the treat from Tennyson, as he from Vergil,
In "Come, O Maid" refashioning the first bucolic.)
The nightingale, the rose aroma gold, the candle
Make harmony in art from utter, outer failure
And thus illuminate the paradox found hinted:
Through self-renunciation you will know fulfilment.

So thoughts that voluntary move harmonious numbers
Enlivened as the nightingale the thought of Milton,
Who, when the wakeful bird sang dark in shady covert
Nocturnal-sweet, could see, though blind, with inward vision,
The emblem of the way that he in bliss had taken:
A light in sound to hear, a higher life in singing.

81. HÁFIZ-HAMMER II.426–28 POEM 67: SAKI BIA KI SCHÜD KADEHĬ LALÈ PÜR ES MEĬ

/xx /xx /xx /xx /xx /x
x/ x/ x/ x/

Innkeeper, here! every chalice of tulip with wine's overbrimming—
So how much more of monkish talk?
Putting all arrogance, flattery out of our thinking, consider:
The kings of China, Rome are—where?
Follow your reason: though birds in the meadow (you hear them?) are drunken,
Alert! the sleep of night is near.
Bough of the springtime, how beauty-endowed is your flexible movement!
Stay safe, I pray, from winter harm.
Comrades, believe me, don't trust to the smoothness of fortune alluring—
A simple faith containing doom.
Houris await us at morn in a field of the Garden of Eden,
And here's the taverner, with glass.
East-wind reminds me of Solomon-time and the Princess of Sheba—
The goblet lend for spirit-cure.
Splendor outspread, and the radiant rose—but a threat is unfolding:
The petals Wind will scatter wide!
Let us drink twice to the welfare of Hátem Thai, wise ruler—
From vain ambition keep us far!
Taking the wine, with the color of scarlet and taste of the sweetest,
Will make my loved one ruddy, sweet.
Carry the pillow outdoors; they are waiting for you in the garden
Already—flute and cedar-tree.
Listen! the singer beginning, the instruments heard in the meadow—
The flute and larger barbiton.
Háfiz, your melody charms are extensively known and well valued
From China to the Grecian fields.

Reply

Tempest may threaten, unsettle the merry, horizon be darkened:
An autumn awe pervades the air.
Weather is melded in portent of storm with a brisk intuition:
The realm is in extreme unease.

Let us but hope that the shah will adhere to the pathway of prudence
    That Hâtem Thai had walked upon.
Even the wisdom of Solomon couldn't prevent him from losing
    The signet ring to Div unblest.
Órmuzd and Áhriman struggled, the spirits of good and of evil—
    The treasure was at length regained.
Ah! but while gone, it had wrought on the lands of the monarch a havoc
    That gladdenened hearts of adder-jinns.
Thus we are wise to be keeping attuned to political breezes—
    For winds may of a sudden shift.
Meanwhile in turning our mood to the pleasanter hues of the morning,
    We favor flute and barbiton,
Timbrel, and lute, and the zither and tympanum, aiding the dancer,
    The singer, and the houri-Muse.
Háfiz, how thrillingly wandering tunes of a Sufi in China
    In mind with Hellene splendors blend:
All is accomplished if only we wisely remember the spreading
    Of Persian verse that you composed
Over the borders and covering continents, aided by currents
    Of wind that bear the poet's breath!

82. HÁFIZ-HAMMER II.456–57 POEM 69: MACHMURĬ DSCHAMĬ ISCHKEM SAKÌ BIDIH SCHERABÌ

/xx /xx /xx /x
        /xx /
/xx /xx /xx /x
        /xx /

Cupbearer drunk on the glass full of loving,
        Hand me the wine!
Fill up the goblet, for how can we revel,
        Dry, at the feast?

See! like the moon are the cheeks of my dearest
        Cloudily veiled:
Play for me, Singer—and, Cupbearer, hand me
        Wine for the song!

Waiting all day for your face in the evening
        Wiped out dismay—
Later enjoyment fills dreaming with pictures
        Only of you.

Ah! at the flash of two eyes I am drunken,
        Where is the cup?
Now I am tearful with gleams of the rubies,
        How can I sleep?

Favor this ring that I give for your necklace:
        Wear it, for me!
Do it, or else I will never know comfort,
        Aid for my pain.

How can you hallow for him, for your loved one,
        Háfiz, your heart?
When did a water mirage in the desert
        Ever refresh?

Reply

One of my friends made a journey to Persia.
        Here's what I learned:
Men in the street, Friday evenings, would gather,
        Avid for song.

There they would improvise fresh entertainment,
        Taking their turns,
Each for the hearers declaiming, from Háfiz,
        Lyrics aflame.

How many men, seven centuries after
        Candle-fire breath
Went into night, will enkindle the people
        Skyward to climb?

83. HÁFIZ-HAMMER II. 484–88 MOGANNINAME: BOOK OF THE SINGER

Moganni gud schaji begül baukĭ rud.

/x /x /x /x

Singer with a tone so noble,
Play the melody, the royal—
Send a novel song to drinkers
And to honor friends departed.

Singer, play the tunes, the cheerful—
Start the singing of the lyric:
See me bent to earth by sorrow,
Lift me up again from kneeling.

Bring a picture from the curtain
Of the Master of the Chamber—
Raising high your voice in triumph,
Set Rahíd or Zohra dancing.

Tap the drum and sound the tympan,
Lend the longed-for tones to comrades—
May their very being deepen,
Strong in thought as in arousal.

Singer, play upon the organ,
Take from hearts all worldly thinking,
May the soul at last be tranquil
When no longer sorrow-spotted.

Come, we have no rending conflict:
Touch the timbrel, not the zither—
If the wine should prove disturbing,
Tamp it down with loud *adufe*.

Singer, come and strike the lute-strings,
Newer melodies beginning—
Heal me with your soothing music,
Heart-woe in the tune dissolving.

Through your fluting be so gracious:
Throw into my heart a flaming!
From myself I'm separated—
Halted now the sorrow-plunder.

Singer, say, where are you hiding?
Play for me another, newer:
When the world's becoming empty
Then the beggar's more than monarch.

Singer, lift the lyre and play it!
Give a means to those without one—
In Iraq the street displaying,
Show the eye the Sindus roadway.

Singer! hear, be quick and busy,
Following the counsel given:
When the woe has overcome me,
Come with fluting, lute, and tabret.

Singer! you're the one I'm trusting,
Play the flute from time to time and
Bring the wine, and if you're saddened,
Blow the pipe—the world is air-breath.

Play the barbiton, O singer!
Fill with wine the empty tankard!
Let us favor shared excitement,
Then enjoy some rest together.

Singer! from the songs I've written
Sing one to the tuneful zither!
Let me sink and ponder, thoughtful,
Then I'll dance in frenzy, naked.

Drunkenness reveals the secret—
Drunks no mystery are guarding.
I am gloomy—play on *two* strings,
Play on *one*, on *three*—keep playing.

Singer! play the tunes, the newer,
Speak to each gazelle when singing:
Cheer the spirit of the heroes,
Joining Bárbüd, Párviz' singer.

More unrest, by fate awakened!—
I—excitement, roguish eyegleams—
All these bloody fields of battle
Drink from inn-flasks, wine-filled, bloody!

Riddling is the course of fortune—
Who'll be biting dust? I wonder.
World-betrayal yet is hidden:
Who can know? the world is gravid.

From the world protect, defend me!
None can dally on a bridgehead:
All this world is but a lodging
Where Giráfiab once conquered—

Just a wasteland, bloodied by the
Sons of Feriddún with armies;
Where is Píran, mighty marshal?
Where is Shida with his dagger?

All their vasty domes are vanished,
No one knows where they are buried.
Fate of one man makes a writer,
Hands another man a dagger.

Reply

What I love about the lyric
At the start is all the varied
Medieval Persian music—
As in Psalm One Hundred Fifty,

We've a listing, quite uncommon,
Of the instrumental blessings,
And if some may prove confounding
("Organ"?) more are full of color.

There's the timbrel, or the tabret,
Or the *duff*, or the *adufe*
(Smaller drum, to which I vary
The synonymous adversions);

And the barbiton (theorbo?)
Legendarily invented
When the chief musician, Bárbüd,
Sought to please the lordly Párviz—

And the bigger drum, the lute or
Likely *oudh*, and then the zither
(To the dulcimer related),
And the frenzy-whipping fluting!

There were times I thought the monarch
Sought for healing of the spirit
As when Saul required of David
Quick relief from utter madness,

And I loved to hear the ruler
So enchanted by the lulling,
Quite beside himself, ecstatic,
Feeling like another person.

But the sovereign of battle,
Fevered ardor reawakened,
Moved by drum and flute and zither,
Soon will fancy he's imbibing

All the bloodiness of battle
Bodied forth in prophet-goblet,
With the world he now imagines
Bursting, birthing mortal peril,

And be terrified and frenzied
Viewing looming parlous carnage
Come to threaten him directly
While he prays for aid, foreseeing

That among the vanished heroes
He ere long may lie reposing—
Vatic, antic, manic, mantic
Sounds the battle-cry in music:

Ulalu! the ruder fluting—
It is not the flute of Rumi,
Into springlike fiery dancing
Blending worshipers in oneness,

But more darkly Dionysal,
With a Bacchic frantic panic
After liberated moments
When he'd thought of dancing naked.

We are moving far from David
With his calming lyre of comfort;
True, he danced before the ark, yet
Undisrobed, although his garments

Seemed disordered, disregarded
When on exiting the temple
He was viewed—a few were startled:
He appeared distraught and shaken.

Fate of one man makes a writer,
Hands another man a dagger.
Here are Háfiz and the Master
Representing both professions—

Friendly, kind conciliation
Which may yet portend a menace:
Shah Namáh is far more tragic
Than a pastoral by Háfiz.

War requires a willing minstrel,
But the epic of our culture
Made me want to turn away from
Everything resembling battle.

Turkestan and fair Bokhara
Háfiz found of lesser value
Than a lover's mark of beauty—
Gracious Tamerlane forgave him

That irreverence in writing.
Ah, but who'll forgive the ruler
Leading youths to die untimely,
While their elders prate of glory!

84. HÁFIZ-HAMMER II.489–503 SAKI-NAMEH: THE BOOK OF TAVERNS

Biarsaki an mei ki hal averd

/x /x /x /x

Bring me, taverner, the vine-juice
That will make us whole, free-giving.
Bring it, pour it, for my heart is
Not free-granting, lacking wholeness.
Bring the wisdom-stone, to make us
Kárun-rich, and old as Noah.
Come, that for your sake be opened
All the gates of life and fortune.
Bring us now, in wet, the fire that
Zoroaster sought in ground-dust.
World and fire-flame veneration,
When we're drunk, are both permitted.
Bring me wine of Jémshid's goblet
Which would gleam in very voidness.
Give it, that I may be strengthened,
Looking through the world as he did.
Taverner! the glass of Jémshid—
Hand me that, and no delaying.
Wisely had he claimed, the monarch,
All the world's not worth a granule.
Taverner!—the nectar goblet!
For to Paradise 'twill lead us.
Flute and lyre proclaim in radiance:
Férment than a crown is finer!
Bring to light the veil-swathed beauty
Prisoned in her narrow dwelling.
Bring her—for I pledge my name to
Wine and goblet benefactions.
Bring to me the flaming water:
Lions drink—and kindle forests!
Lend it, let me storm the heavens,
Rend the world-wolf's net asunder!
Wine, whereby the houris teach the
Angels Eden-like behavior!

On the heat-glow I'm depending,
Airing out my brain with fragrance.
Bring me wine, whereof the splendor
Gleamings gave to Jem and Khósru.
Give!—with flute would I be singing:
Where is Jem, and where is Ká'us?
Blessing bring of ancient ages,
Bless the shahs that long have left us.
Wine, that mastery will give and
Purity to hearts is preaching,
Bring to me, the shah of hearts, for
Now I'm not myself in spirit.
Give me wine, and wash me pure of
Spot and taint of care and worry.
Grant—and view the face of gladness.
Gloomed, I crave a treasured wisdom.
Dwelling in a spirit garden,
Why am I enchained and fettered?
When a glass of wine I'm holding,
All the world that mirror shows me.
Then I, beggar, speak of lordship!
Háfiz, waking up, is singing,
In her sphere, Zohré rejoices.
Fear the day unstable, shifting:
From the wine entreat more life-time!
For the wine is life-increasing,
Opening the gates of myst'ry.
Gather, taverner, the drinkers,
For the world to all is faithless.
Memory will bubbles lend that
Vanish like the crown of Kóbad.
Seek in wine your heart-fulfilment,
You've no peace of mind if wineless.
Like the body reft of spirit
Is the heart whence wine is taken.
Taverner! brim up the goblets,
Let me tell of royal greatness.
Taverner! the world's inconstant,
With a will to shed your heart-blood.
Taverner! don't give us problems,
You're not fire- but earth-created.

Fill the goblet up with wine, then,
Free of dregs and fresh and cleanly.
Give me some with sweeter spices,
Gold and silver I am lacking.
Give me of the ruby-colored,
Needing neither lies nor boasting.
Lend the coral prayer bead-chain
As a pledge of wine, her blessing.
Near the "cloister" is the tavern:
Many treasures there are buried.
Should one tell you, "Stay, don't *go* there,"
Give him a "Good-night" for answer.
Bring me, host, the purple goblet,
Heart and spirit gladness granting,
That my sorrows' hold be loosened,
Leading me to firmer pathways.
Bring the wine, our souls' nutrition,
Powering the heart and spirit.
I this world would fain be leaving:
Bring the goblet's moon- and sunlight,
That in heav'n my throne be readied.
Come with goblet-wine, the oldest—
Gradually make me drunken.
If with purest wine you treat me,
Drunken will I sing, and grateful.
Taverner! your cheeks the fragrance
Waft as of a vernal férment.
Take the glass, no sin be fearing:
Wine's in Paradise decanted.
Come, I need some wine, and badly:
Put into my hand a goblet.
Of the world's ill fate despairing,
I've been running to the "cloister."
Hand me happy-making wine, and
I'll bestride my battle-charger,
Rustum-like head down the highroad,
Seeking heart-air in the tumble.
Give the ruby goblet which the
Heart in timely wise will open,
So will Reason's rule be countered
And in worlds be banners planted.

With the goblet's aid, caressing,
We will quell the flame of sorrow.
Let us drink today together—
There's no other time so fitting.
Who the festival have ordered
Are with happy mind contented,
All the snares of Divs evading,
Envied by the dust below them.
Who has such a throne established
Of a little ten-day corner?
Youth, alas! in wind evanished!
Blesséd, who have spent it wisely!
Give me wine, and overleaping
Both the worlds, I'll fly in oneness.
Quickly give me *kótel*-measure,
Openly or else in secret.
Elephants big drums may carry,
But departure-drum has sounded.
From the light-sphere comes at morning
Call of houris to me clearly:
"Lovely bird, and sweeter spirit,
Lift your pinions, break the cages,
Sit upon the seven-dóme-roof
Where the spirits are reposing."
At the time of Bisurdshímir
Menutshír wins all with beauty.
Nushirmán upon his goblet
Had this writ in early ages:
"Counsel hear from us, and learn of
How the course of life is fated.
Here is but a vale of sorrow,
Few the joys in realm sublunar.
We are glad when cares are banished—
Who has nothing, has no worries."
Where is Jem, and where his goblet?
Solomon, and where his mirror?
What philosopher's aware of
When Jem, Ká'us, had existed?
When they from the world departed,
Naught but names they left behind them.
Do not bind your heart to earth, for

Once you're gone, there's no returning.
Fools alone their hearts have given
To the earth, to heaven alien.
She will never lend what's wished for;
Here is not the place of gladness.
Taverner, the fiery water!—
Let my burning be extinguished.
For my heart in flame is lying—
Therefore liquid pour upon it.
Taverner, give ruby-water
That the ruby's hue has stolen.
Quickly give us aqua vitae,
Flowing like the heated sunglow.
Single glass will let you see the
Five high cupolas, nine stepways.
Unsupported they can go there
Who annihilate the selfhood.
If you're clever, be quite simple,
Like the pub dust, nothing higher:
Be not bound to earthly cloister,
Or like dust you'll soon be scattered.
Give me, host, the royal goblet
That the heart and spirit gladdens:
Wine and goblet nothing mean but
Purest love, as we are speaking.
As the lightning, youth will vanish—
As the wind our life, soon over—
Leave behind the six-doored dwelling
And the old nine-headed serpent,
Gold and mind expending nimbly
If you still can love the spirit.
Hasten to the other lifeworld!
All but God is vain and idle.
Give me, host, the spirit jewel,
Physic lend the heart that's wounded—
After Jem had lost his goblet
All the universe turned useless.
Give me, host, the crystal goblet,
Wake with wine the heart that's deadened.
Every clump of loam beneath could

Be the skull of Alexander.
Seas are but the blood of princes,
Desert-dust the dust of beauties,
So a vineyard venerator
Stated, in his hand a goblet:
Here below, our fate will flatter,
Joying no one but the foolish.
Give me drink that's light and bitter!
Friendly hand the bitter sweetens.
There was more than one Daríus
Who the world entire had mastered,
But because they're dead and buried
You believe them quite fictitious.
Go, my host, to see the shah, and
Say, "O Shah, like Jem encrownéd,
Seek the heart of simple people,
Then the glass, that worlds can show you.
From the earth our empty sorrow
You can drive away, wine-aided
In this time of throne's adornment,
Fruit of royalty to gather."
Lord of earth and prince of seasons,
Moon of fortune, mighty monarch,
Whose refulgent crown has granted
Tranquil rest to fish and bird-life,
Heart, eye-brightness of the blessed,
Lord of grace, of hearts the master,
Nourisher of faith and world-king,
To the throne adornment lending,
Of this ruler how to speak, then?—
Reason halting in amazement.
For his power knows no limit—
Weakened, see, my head is sinking
As I lift my hand in prayer,
Turn my face to the Creator:
"Lord my God, by all your graces,
By your name, its holy secrets,
And your word in truth eternal,
By your gifts divinely sanctioned,
Sovran of the world make happy,

Aid his throne and crown, adorn them,
Just and unjust rightly ruling,
Granting signs of heaven's favor."
Shah Mansúr the world be leading,
Dusty sorrow far be flying!
God be praised! You, Jem-ring bearer,
Are of world and faith a hero,
Rightly named as rich in vict'ry,
Foes in every case defeated—
Feriddún-like ever festive,
Rustum-like on field of battle.
Monarchs never have resembled
These but you, O pearl of heaven!
Franks pay tribute with their jewels,
As do Abyssinian rulers.
Turks, Chinese, and Jews alike are
To your signet-ring subjected—
Swarthy Saturn made your servant,
And your slave the very heaven.
And the phoenix of your tent will
Guard our earth-world with his pinions.
Greater yet than Alexander,
Yours are lands from Greece to China.
Long remain in rightful station—
All the hidden things uncover.
Shoreless, wide the sea of praises—
I must limit now my prayers.
From the poems of Nizami,
Oratoric art's adornment,
I will cite three fitting verses,
Finer than of pearls the purest:

Far more countries may you conquer
Than you ever would have dreamt of!
May the highest fortune lend you
Day by day renewing triumphs.
And the wine, the spirit healer,
To your health I'm humbly drinking.

Reply

We've the storming of the heaven
With the world-beast wide a-gaping
And the kindling of the forest
By the fiery lions' rising
With the fierce nine-headed serpent
And the six-doored realm defeated
While the surging sweep of trochees
That a pre-creating chaos
Can preserve by fermentation
In the human soul upwelling
Through exuberant arousal
From unsoundable abysses
With sublimity of crimson
Hymns the vast "I am" of singing.

85.–87. HÁFIZ-HAMMER II.522 QUATRAINS 6, 7, 8

/xx /xx /xx /xx /xx /x
/xx /xx / – /xx /xx /

VI. Si an badei dirinei dihkan perverd

Give me the good olden wine of the sort that has nourished the farmer,
Handing the goblet to me, feeling the time rushing by.
Make me so drunk I become unaware of whatever's occurring—
You, you alone I will tell all of the secrets of life.

VII. Ei auki nichend mihr u mah es temkin

You are the one whom the moon and the sun in their splendor majestic
Daily and nightly revere, humbly bowed down in the dust.
Why do you sit there constrained in the heart and the tongue and
hand-shackled?
Crush not the glory below, neither be idle and still.

VIII. Ba dost nischin ve badei dscham taleb

Sociably sit with your friends and companions, and ask for the wineglass,
Only one kiss to demand—take, from the cypress nearby.
If when afflicted and wounded a sufferer seeks for a healing,
Say that the lancet may be just what the doctor would use.

Reply

Classic Ovidian distichs we hear, though *in medio aevo*,
Timeless the elegy old, antic the folly remains.
Men will commiserate, sharing their sorrows—how little they differ!
Two are not readily one, save in a moment of grace.

Quatrain the first is but friendly and kindly, and kindness-inviting,
Strophe the second reveals reverence, empathy too,
Stanza the third might apply to the mute addressee or the speaker:
"Hair of the dog" which had bit, hangover-wisdom for love.

Weary the feeling and soothing as well in the swell of the lilting—
Pause for a breath if you will, here before taking a drink.
Waves of the water of life overwelling the wet and the thirsty
Whelm us and yet we may glide, vim over-brimming our woe.

89.–91. HÁFIZ-HAMMER II.523, 525 QUATRAINS 10, 11, 16

/xx /xx /xx /xx /xx /x
/xx /xx / – /xx /xx /

X. NE DEVLETĬ DÜNJA BESITEM MI ERSED

Bliss of our world, and no other? Too dear for the burden of worry,
All our existence' delight never outweighing the pain.
Sev'n thousand years of the tumult of pleasure and blessedness never
Adequate payment would be meriting seven days' grief.

XI. IMSCHEB SI GHAMET MIJANĬ CHUN CHAHEM CHUFT

All of tonight will I spend bleeding tears for the pain you inflicted—
Throwing the pillow of health far as I can in my woe.
Send me, I beg of you, only for comfort, the image I dream of—
Then, though if merely in dream, you are beside me in bed.

XVI. GÜFTI KI TÜRA SCHEVEM MÜDAR ENDISCHE

"Always," you said to me, "I will be thinking of you and stay faithful.
Now, in your heart, be serene—keep yourself patient and calm.
Patience, you know, is the primary virtue of heart-grateful lovers."
One little glow-drop—for that, myriad thanks will you have.

Reply

Brevity-gems, the compression of craft made them pledges of blessing—
Cameo-testament more lasting than Solomon's seal.
Waters will never quench love, nor will floods of apocalypse drown it—
Love is the fire of our life, sent through the air from the Eye.

Birds pour their hearts out to love, 'mid the dew of the early-come dawning—
Bright-eyed, the light of the sky filling their psalming with fire—
Clearer than laughter, exalted, as water from silver-gilt pitcher
Poured for the steed of the Sun, rider awake for the race.

You are the length of our days, and our stay in a moment of trial—
Almond-tree, asked about love, straightaway blossomed and gleamed.
Ever the face of the lover will radiate light of the morning—
Evening but deepening love: Zohra, Messiah at one.

92.–95. HÁFIZ-HAMMER II.524–25 QUATRAINS 12, 13, 14, 17

/xx /xx /xx /xx /xx /x
/xx /xx / – /xx /xx /

XII. Der arsui bus u kenaret mürdem

Out of a longing for kisses, embraces, I've died, I will say it.
 Yes, I have died of desire, wanting your ruby-smooth lips.
Yet I am chatting too much, I had better explain it quite briefly:
 You must return; he awaits—one who has many times died.

XIII. Dschana tschu schebì ba tu burus averdem

I have extended this night, O my Love, till it's blended with morning:
 When I'm with *you* it is so—say I'm no man if I lie.
Death can in future no longer infuse me with frail trepidation:
 I flowing life have imbibed, fresh from your ruby-like lips.

XIV. Ta kai bud in dschevr u dschef kerdeni tu

Tell me how long you'll continue to smite us with hard perturbation,
 Pain to keep giving to those guiltless in mind and in heart.
Look at the blood-spotted sword in the hand of the plagued ones, offended—
 Should it come near to your neck, it will be streaming with blood.

XVII. Ischkĭ ruhĭ jar ber men nesar megir

Hold me not back from the love of the cheeks of the friend that I cherish—
 One who is ill in the heart tell not of pointless detail.
You will be wise if aware of the ways of experienced people:
 Punish not one who is drunk. Gossipy anecdotes?—no!

Reply

Ars amatoria? Psychoanalysis here, in abundance!
 Frustrated love turned to hate, punishing self, then the Friend.
Love-drunk the poet, unguarded, lays bare the heart's devious turning:
 Many times martyred, he burns—now revolution will burst!

Strophe the first—an example of self-sacrificial despairing;
        Stanza the second—reverse: gratitude, worship, and love.
Lyric the third is a terror; the poet, a nation rebellious.
        Lastly, a "marital spat"—blunt in reproachful command.

96.–98. HÁFIZ-HAMMER II.530–31 QUATRAINS 32, 33, 34

/xx /xx /xx /xx /xx /x
/xx /xx / – /xx /xx /

XXXII. Ba mai be kenarĭ dschui mi bajed bud

It is befitting to stay on the bank of a stream with a wine-flask,
Washing the sorrow-filled breast, making it free of its woe.
We, like the rose, only ten days of life, all too brief, are allotted,
Let us then face it with cheer, and with a smile on our lips.

XXXIII. Ei scherbem sede ghondscha mestur es tu

Rosebuds are shutting their chalices—you have embarrassed them deeply.
Hyacinth-glow guttered out, wholly extinguished by you.
Ha! but what base to compare? for the roses and you differ greatly:
They are made bright by the sun—sunlight shines brightly through you.

XXXIV. Ewel bewefaï wisalem der dad

High did I raise up my head at the start with the joy of contentment,
Now nothing more can I lift, saving the calyx of woe—
Streams flooding down from the eyes, and a flaming consuming my heart-blood,
She, like the dust of the road throwing me out to the wind.

Reply

Quatrain-kaleidoscope, here are the highs and the lows of emotion
Striking the soul of the one vulnerable to her will.
Falling in love means agreeing that you are a woundable person:
Fine is the courage in this—living in truth, not a lie.

Open your heart to the world, to the sun and the storm and the sorrow:
Yes, to the rain and the earth, ev'n to the dust of the road.
You are the soil and the water, the air and the fire and the spirit
Come from the world of the stars, part of their burning and whirl.

99.–101. HÁFIZ-HAMMER II.553, 568, 572 MOKATAAT: FRAGMENTS

X. Ber tu chuanem si defterĭ achlak

x/ x/ x/ x/ x/x
x/ x/ x/ x/ x/

The verse from *Book of Virtues* will I read you
Of faithfulness and magnanimity—
Who has not torn your heart with grievous trouble,
A lode of gold him grant, and more beside.
Don't leave the tree that offered shade and shelter—
Give fruits to them that showered you with stones.
Large-heartedness learn well: the humble oyster
Will give a pearl to one who risked a life.

XXXII. Ejamĭ behar est u gul u lale u nesrin

/xx /xx /xx /xx /xx /x
/xx /xx / – /xx /xx /

(These two distichs Háfiz dedicated to his young son, who had died.)

Days of the spring have arrived, with the violet, tulip, the roses,
        Sprouting up high from the dust, where you are lying in dust.
I will lament at the grave as a cloud of the spring on a meadow,
        Weep till you sprout from the dust, higher than flower of spring.

XLII Dila didì ki an fersane fersend

x/ x/ x/ x/ x/x
x/ x/ x/ x/ x/

Consider, heart, how odd the lot appointed
By motley Fate, in playing. For this youth
Hugged to his breast no breast of alabaster
But had above his head a marble slab.

Reply

Who've the lore of winning tone
Nevermore will live alone:
In my ear and spirit dwell
That I may of Eden tell.

Ethics and an elegy,
Then the laugh of liberty,
You to echo every mood
Were by heaven's will endued.

Tulip, violet, and rose,
Háfiz, you're aligned with those
Who until the close of day
Wash the stain of woes away.

102.–103. HÁFIZ-HAMMER II.554, 555 FRAGMENTS

XIII. Shaha mubschiri si bihischtem reside est

x/ x/ x/ x/ x/ x/

These tidings had I heard, O Shah, from Paradise:
With houri-beauty, like the fount of Sélsebil,
Would come a youth well-grown, sweet-worded, deep in mind,
And sweet and gracious, with a fine, light-hearted wit.
Of course I asked him then, "Pray tell me why you're here."
He answered, "On the Shah's behalf, who's angel-like.
He used to love my talk, but now he's merely bored.
So I appeal to you to come—fulfil his wish."

XIV. Der in sulmet sera ta kei bebui dost binischinem

/xx /xx /xx /xx /xx /x
/xx /xx / – /xx /xx /

Shall I continue to sit in the darkness and long for the comrade,
  Now with a finger in mouth, now bending head to the knee?
Patience I've long ago lost—only wolf, and no lion, appearing—
  Intellect wandering round—ravens have scattered the doves.
Come then, you bird out of Eden, and grant me some happier tidings:
  Maybe with time will return earlier people one liked.

Reply

They're a kaleidoscope, forty-four fragments that Hammer selected.
  Suddenly interest begins: maybe a link will appear?
Yes!—I can sense a connection, ambivalent, comforting-troubling:
  Solitude's driven him mad—therefore he'll conjure a "dream."
Lofty, angelic, the ruler will likely require panegyric—
  Payment for favors? what kind? Tricky is living "in style."

Selected Bibliography

Arberry, Arthur J. 1962. *Fifty Poems of Hafiz: Texts and Translations Collected and Made, Introduced and Annotated by Arthur J. Arberry*. Cambridge: Cambridge University Press.

Bidney, Martin. 2007. *A Poetic Dialogue with Adam Mickiewicz: The "Crimean Sonnets."* Bonn: Bernstein-Verlag.

———. April 23–24, 2009. "Crossing Borders: Goethe's Medieval Middle Eastern Wine." Paper presented at "'In Vino Veritas': A Symposium on Wine and the Influence of Bacchus from Classical Antiquity through the Eighteenth Century," Center for Medieval and Early Renaissance Studies, Binghamton University, Binghamton, New York. (Several of the points in the "Introduction" first appeared here.)

———. 2010. *East-West Poetry: A Western Poet Responds to Islamic Tradition in Sonnets, Hymns, and Songs*. East-West Bridge Builders 1. Binghamton, NY: Global Academic Publishing.

Emerson, Ralph Waldo. 1986. *The Poetry Notebooks of Ralph Waldo Emerson*. Edited by Ralph H. Orth, Albert J. von Frank, Linda Allandt, and David W. Hill. Columbia: University of Missouri Press.

Goethe, Johann Wolfgang von. 1998. *Sämtliche Werke nach Epochen seines Schaffens*. Münchner Ausgabe. Vol. 11.1.2 of *West-östlicher Divan*. Edited by Karl Richter, with Katharina Mommsen and Peter Ludwig. Munich: Hanser.

———. 2010. *West-East Divan: The Poems, with "Notes and Essays": Goethe's Intercultural Dialogues*. Translated by Martin Bidney ("Divan," with commentary poems) and Martin Bidney and Peter Anton von Arnim ("Notes and Essays"). East-West Bridge Builders 2. Albany: State University of New York Press. (Recitations from poems 5, 26, and 128 can be heard on BBC 3: *Twenty Minutes*, "Episode 1 of 2: Goethe and the West-Eastern Divan," July 21, 2012, 8:35 pm; 191, 193, 233, 197 (in that order) on BBC 3: *Twenty Minutes*, "Episode 2 of 2: Goethe and the West-Eastern Divan," July 23, 2012, 8:40 pm; seven poems and several replies are recited by the translator on diwans.org.)

Hafis, Mohammed Schemsed-din. (1814) 1973. *Der Diwan: Aus dem Persichen zum erstenmal ganz übersetzt von Joseph von Hammer-Purgstall.* Facsimile edition. 2 vols. Hildesheim: George Olms Verlag.

Hafiz, Muhammad Shemseddin. 1928. *Poems from the Divan of Hafiz.* Translated by Gertrude Lowthian Bell. 2nd ed. London: Heinemann.

Hammer[-Purgstall], Joseph von. 1818. *Geschichte der schönen Redekünste Persiens, mit einen Blütenlese aus 200 persischen Dichtern.* Vienna.

Loloi, Parvin. 2004. *Hâfiz, Master of Persian Poetry: A Critical Bibliography. English Translations since the Eighteenth Century.* London: I. B. Tauris in association with the Iran Heritage Foundation.

Mommsen, Katharina. 2001. *Goethe und der Islam.* Frankfurt am Main: Insel Verlag.

Mommsen, Katharina. 2010. *Keine Rettungsmittel als die Liebe: Schillers und Goethes Bündnis im Spiegel ihrer Dichtungen.* Göttingen: Wallstein Verlag.

Wohlleben, Joachim. 2004. *Die Ghaselen des Hafiz: Neu in deutsche Prosa übersetzt, mit Einleitung und Lesehilfen von Joachim Wohlleben.* Würzburg: Königshausen & Neumann.

Index